Let Them Come

ANDREA COLSON

DEDICATION

In loving memory of 2-S

My Sunday school lost a little angel,
but heaven gained one.

CONTENTS

*"But Jesus called them unto Him, and said,
'Suffer little children to come unto Me, and forbid them not:
for of such is the kingdom of God.'"*
Luke 18:16

1 EVERY WEEK AN ADVENTURE

I have been a missionary practically my whole life. My family went to Hawaii as missionaries when I was a little girl, and that was where we first met people from Chuuk, Micronesia. Several years later our family moved to Chuuk and we have lived here as missionaries ever since. After graduating from high school and college, I knew in my heart that the Lord was not finished using me as a missionary and that He still had a job for me to do in Chuuk. So I joined Central Missionary Clearinghouse and began raising my own missionary support, mostly through friends in America that sponsor me by giving to my account at CMC each month.

The Lord has been very good to me. It is wonderful to do what you love and love what you do. Thanks mainly to email, Facebook, and my personal blog, I have many friends around the world who love seeing the pictures and stories I post from Chuuk almost daily. I am glad to share what is happening in

1

this beautiful but remote part of the world.

Probably my favorite part of being a missionary is that you never know what might happen next, or what adventure you may stumble into today. My first book, *Reaching the Uttermost Part*, tells mostly about the adventures I have had on mission trips to Chuuk's outer islands. Sometimes I surprise myself when I think about the things I have actually done and seen! But even a normal day can be an adventure in the life of a missionary, at least if you live in Chuuk. My grand-scale adventures may be stories of long ocean voyages to visit tiny coral islands, but my weekly adventures have proven to be just as exciting (and dangerous).

Every week my brother Matthew and I drive to the far end of our island to Kinisou Baptist Church in Wichap Village. This church was started by Baptist missionaries years ago. Over time, missionaries came and went until the Chuukese folks were left without a missionary at all. When their Chuukese pastor died, the church family was alone and sad. Matthew stepped up and offered to be their missionary, and the Lord has blessed in so many ways since then.

I teach the children and Matthew is the church pastor. In our first service at Kinisou Baptist we had eight people, including Matthew and me. Now we regularly have ten or fifteen times that many folks in church on Sunday and during the week for children's Bible school or "kinter." We record Matthew's sermons and my Sunday School lessons and play them on our radio station, and the folks in church record songs. The kids especially love learning the new songs I write and teach them, and have livened up our radio schedule quite a bit. What they lack in tone they make up for in enthusiasm. One of their favorite songs is to the tune of "Children, Go Where I Send Thee" and names all Ten Commandments, starting with Commandment #1 until we finally repeat all ten commandments, backwards, the last time through. Many radio listeners have told us how much they enjoy tuning in to hear what is happening at the Baptist church in Wichap this week.

I teach the boys and girls Bible stories using my big flannel graph board and felt pictures. Many of the children never heard stories from the Old Testament before coming to our church. One hundred-and-fifty pairs of eyes were glued to the flannel graph board the afternoon I told them the story of Daniel in the lions' den. They were certain that was the most exciting adventure story they had ever heard, until the next week when we learned about Jonah and the whale!

After our Bible lesson, I play my ukulele and we sing our invitation song, "I Have Decided to Follow Jesus." Many of the children and teenagers from Wichap and the next village Epinup have been saved during "kinter" at the Baptist church.

One afternoon a lady came to church looking for her little boy. She had searched everywhere for him but he was nowhere to be found. Her neighbors told her, "Go check the Baptist church. All the kids go there for Bible class." Sure enough, she walked into church and there was her little boy sitting on the front row, listening to a Bible story. The relieved mother told me later that she knew exactly how Mary and Joseph must have felt when they looked frantically for Jesus and found him in church.

The ride to Wichap is very rough, which makes the

four-mile drive take around forty-five minutes each way. Even the paved sections of road are cracked in places, full of potholes and deep trenches. The paved road runs out before we reach Wichap, and from that point the drive is literally off-road; a winding, rocky, muddy path that leads down by the ocean and up around the side of a mountain. Every time we turn the corner and finally reach the village, we are met by groups of kids jumping up and down and waving because they are so excited to see the truck!

For years one of our little boys had a dog, Osenimu, who was our self-appointed guide-dog. As soon as the truck stopped at his house and the kids climbed on board, Osenimu would run out in front of us and lead the truck down the road and up the hill to the church. Whenever we would stop to pick up more boys and girls, Osenimu patiently waited for the truck to get going again so he could continue to escort us the rest of the way. During the church service, Osenimu usually stayed outside and took a nap in the shade under the truck, but sometimes the rascal would sneak inside the building and stretch out underneath one of the church benches. As soon as church let out, Osenimu would run to the bottom of the hill and wait to lead us back down the road to his house, where he and the kids eagerly waited for the next church day.

I hate having to write about Osenimu in the past tense, but sadly our happy guide dog who loved church so much was killed one afternoon when a mean person struck him with a machete for no reason. Chuuk is a dangerous place, and usually the violence is senseless and random like what happened to our church dog. Even now I miss seeing

4

Osenimu running ahead of us down the village road, stopping to look behind him every now and then just to make sure we are keeping up.

****

One afternoon a little boy hopped on the back of the truck with his friends who had invited him to come to church. His name was Chiper, and he was so excited to finally be going to a place he had only ever heard about: the Baptist church with Andrea and Matthew! Since that first day Chiper comes to church faithfully, and brings his little brother Dainer with him. Every Sunday and Tuesday, no matter how early we drive by, there are Chiper and Dainer waiting for us with their friends underneath the mango tree. They see the truck and come running!

Chiper and Dainer's daddy passed away a few months before they started coming to church. He was known throughout the village as a bad man and an alcoholic. He left his wife and little boys and built himself a shack way up on top of the mountain, where he would spend his time making home-made liquor. One day a man walked up to the door and called out for a drink. When there was no answer, he peeked in the window. There was Chiper and Dainer's daddy lying on the floor of his house. He had died several days before, but nobody knew.

After he asked Jesus to come into his heart, Chiper wanted to get baptized. Before we built a baptistry in the church, we would go down to the ocean and baptize there. One Sunday morning after church, everyone who could fit piled on the back of the truck and inside the cab while the others walked alongside, and we went a mile down the road to the beach where we could have a baptismal service. That week a box of children's clothes had come in the mail from a friend in America. Chiper was very excited to get baptized wearing his new church clothes, a long sleeve shirt and a little pair of black pants.

Chiper wants to be a preacher when he grows up. One time when he heard his friends talking about what they wanted to be when they got older, he asked them, "You mean you guys don't want to be preachers?" He could not imagine wanting to be anything else!

Each week I try to teach the children lessons that will help them grow up loving Jesus and living for Him. One day our lesson to memorize was from Dr. Homer Lindsay, Jr., the pastor of First Baptist Church in Jacksonville, Florida:

God wants me to:
1) Love Jesus
2) Be thankful
3) Be a soul-winner

Another week we learned a lesson I had read that morning in my "Experiencing God" daily devotional book by Henry Blackaby. The two most important things in life are to love Jesus and to do what He says. If you get these two principles right and live by them each day, you will be living your life exactly the way God wants.

One time we learned about the ten lepers that Jesus healed, but only one of them came back to say thank you. I told the kids that our assignment that month was to write a list of one hundred things we are thankful for. For weeks, everyone, including the adults, worked on writing thank-you lists. On Sunday morning everyone who had turned in their list that week came forward and received a gold medal and a cupcake. They were thrilled! (Some of the kids even wrote a second list of a hundred things so they could get another cupcake.)

Myreen was thankful for her eyelashes that keep dust and sand out of her eyes, and for the ocean where she can get food to eat. She was thankful for the times she is sick, because she can pray and ask God to heal her.

Atame had a long list of a hundred different things, including his ukulele, his Bible, his fishing line, his canoe, his pitcher, his towel, Jesus, his fork and spoon, and his tin roof. His niece Edwick handwrote her own thank-you list of one hundred things, like her favorite foods: octopus, breadfruit, apples, and bananas; and her favorite animals: dogs, cats, pigs, chickens, monkeys, and horses (she has never actually seen the last two kinds of animals on her list in person, she only knows about them from the story of Noah's ark).

Keireen is blind in one eye and comes to church faithfully, toting her baby sister on her hip most of the time. She finished her list of things she is thankful for by writing, "My radio, earrings, necklace, flip-flops, and Andrea."

You can see why going to Wichap is the highlight of my week.

Sunday morning song service at Kinisou Baptist Church

Matthew baptizing Friday in our church baptistry

Matthew with a truckload of kids coming to church

Each week I teach the children at Bible Baptist Church and Kinisou Baptist Church a story from the Bible

How exciting to hear the story of Daniel in the lions' den for the first time

"Turn in your Bibles to…"

S-Bo and our new church dog, Okasi

2 COCONUTS AND BIRTHDAY CAKES

Even though Wichap and Epinup are on Weno, the center island in the Chuuk Lagoon, both villages remind me of life on an outer island. The people are very poor and some of them rarely leave that side of the island, since most families do not own a vehicle and they have to walk or catch a ride on the taxi-flatbed if they want to go anywhere. Ladies from Wichap come to town every day to sell fresh coconuts, local food and flower leis and make enough money to buy rice for their families. Many of the men are fishermen, and others grow gardens or work in the taro patch. Even though our island has a small power plant, most homes in Wichap and Epinup do not have electricity. There is no real sewer system out there since not all the pipes and drains were ever installed. A lot of old equipment is still sitting beside the road, like a dump truck, a tractor and a backhoe.

11

Whoever was in charge of putting in the sewer lines and paving the road must have decided the job was too hard and walked away leaving everything behind for the weeds to grow over and the kids to play on. The high cab of the rusty tractor makes a good lookout point on Sunday morning when the little boys are trying to see if that is Matthew's truck coming down the road!

One Sunday morning before church, Matthew sat underneath the mango tree by the side of the road and played his guitar. A group of boys from the village soon gathered around to listen and watch. They had never seen anyone play bluegrass-style before! When Matthew finished amazing them with his fast guitar playing, he invited everyone to come with him to church. All the boys trooped in together and sat on the two front benches. That morning was probably the first time many of them had ever been to church.

One of the boys was 12-year-old BR, whose family lives up on the mountainside. Something about BR really touched my heart. He was thin and dressed in raggedy clothes, and had big serious eyes. After that first Sunday, BR began coming to church faithfully. He loved learning about Jesus and the Bible and would bring his younger brothers and sisters with him. One morning after Sunday School, BR prayed with me and asked Jesus to come into his heart. That year on Christmas Day, BR brought Matthew and me a rice sack full of coconuts that he had picked off a tree and husked all by himself. What a big job for a little boy! When I saw his bag of coconuts, I remembered the story I heard once about a boy in Africa who walked for miles to get a special seashell for his missionary. The missionary felt bad because the boy had walked so far just to bring him a present, but the boy smiled and said, "Long walk part of gift!"

Christmas Day also happens to be little Gloria's birthday. That same Christmas I made a birthday cake and wrote "Happy Birthday Jesus & Gloria" on it. Gloria was so excited! In January I kept the project going and started making birthday cakes for all my kids on their special day. Soon the adults began letting me know *their* birthdays, too. With as many folks as we have in church, almost every week at least one person will be celebrating a birthday. Some days I take five or six birthday cakes with us in the truck. Because of the bumpy ride, the hardest part of the job is getting the cakes from my kitchen table all the way out to Wichap with no accidents along the way. Thankfully, everybody is always so excited to finally get their own birthday cake that no one minds a little smeared icing.

At first, I made traditional two-layer cakes, but after having several cakes split in half along the way, I switched to making bundt cakes instead. The hole in the middle is the perfect size for a paper cup with a special birthday surprise, like a toy car, a small stuffed animal or some hair barrettes. Friends in America saw pictures of our birthday boys and girls on my Facebook page and started sending me boxes of cake mixes, sprinkles, powdered sugar and Crisco for the icing. What a big help!

One Sunday, I brought a birthday cake for KJ, but was surprised to see that he was not in church that morning. After Sunday School, KJ's sister told me that her brother was in the hospital. Several months before, KJ's family had all been diagnosed with MDR (multiple-drug resistant) TB. The whole family spent several weeks in the TB isolation ward at the Chuuk State Hospital. Finally, they were allowed to go back home, and the hospital's mobile clinic would come check on them every few weeks and make sure they were taking their medicine. That week when the doctor made his regular house call, he said that KJ and his dad had to go back to the hospital for more treatment. KJ was devastated! For weeks he had been looking forward to getting his first birthday cake ever, and now he was headed back to the isolation ward.

KJ's sister took his cake for him so their mama could take it to the hospital that evening. The next day my dad and I went up to the hospital to check on KJ. The nurse in charge of the TB ward gave us face masks to wear so we could go back to where the patients stay. There is a little covered-porch area where the TB patients can sit outside behind the hospital, and KJ met us there. He could not wait to tell me that he got his birthday cake, and was just as excited about the portable radio I brought him. One week after our children's Bible lesson, KJ came forward during the invitation and prayed to receive Jesus. Sitting together underneath the tin-roof porch behind the hospital, KJ and I both prayed that he would get better soon and be able to come back to church.

I missed seeing KJ's sincere face in Sunday School and church. He loved watching me tell Bible stories using my flannel graph pictures and always sat in the middle of the front row, listening intensely. Two months went by, then the doctors said that KJ was well enough to go home. That week when Matthew and I rolled up to the church in the truck, there was KJ smiling and waving with all the other kids. What a blessing to see his happy face! His little cousin Omwusom came with him, and during the invitation both boys stood up. KJ told me that Omwusom had been looking forward to coming to "kinter" at the Baptist church all day long, and had planned to come forward in the invitation and pray to receive Jesus. When we finished praying together, Omwusom was so excited he could hardly contain himself!

One Tuesday afternoon, I took a birthday cake with me to Wichap for little MK. He looked so pitiful in his birthday picture. His arms and hands were covered with scars and he was wearing a girl's shirt that was too big for him. He loved the toy car that came with his cake, and his older cousins were more than happy to make sure he carried his birthday cake home safely. When we got home that evening I found a box waiting for me that a friend in America sent, full of little boys' clothes! Once again God's timing was perfect, now MK could get some much-needed new clothes on Sunday.

Before I started teaching Sunday School, I asked if anybody had seen MK yet. His cousins all said that he was on his way, and they were happy to hear that I had something special for him. Finally, here came little MK. I gave him his new shorts and t-shirts, and we put his new clothes in a bag. He was so excited, and everybody in church was just as happy for him. We actually got to see him smile at last!

One of the families in our church is from Epinup and lives in a little shack up on the mountainside. Bisina is the grandmother, and she brings her grown children and grandchildren with her to church every week. One of Bisina's youngest granddaughters is Bisiann, a sweet little thing who is partially blind. Bisiann loves to come to church with her brothers and sisters, and always sits so still and listens to the Bible story.

On Sunday morning, Bisiann's older brother, Arson, came up to me as soon as church was over and told me that Bisiann's birthday was that week. I wrote her name down on my calendar, and promised to bring her cake with me on Tuesday afternoon. Bisiann was so excited about her birthday cake! As soon as we closed in prayer on Tuesday, I gathered all the kids together and we went outside to take birthday pictures. Bisiann is used to reaching out for whoever is nearby so she can have someone to follow. She caught hold of my jean skirt and followed me outside while I carried her birthday cake and presents, a pink-and-white toy puppy and a new pair of pink flip-flops. What an adorable smile our little blind birthday girl had on her sweet face! As soon as we finished taking pictures, Arson came to help her put on her new shoes. She had come to church barefooted that day, so the pink flip-flops that a friend in America had sent were the perfect present. Arson carried Bisiann's cake and carefully led her down the hill and back home again, like the good brother he is. Watching the two of them reminded me once again just how very blessed I am to be these little children's missionary.

Happy Birthday to Bisiann, Enina and Joy-M

Arson keeping a protective eye out for his sister Bisiann

ANDREA COLSON

18

3 MY "TINY TIM"

Every time we drive into Wichap, we pass the grave
of a little boy named SST. I met SST and his mom
on hospital visitation one Saturday morning. SST was
13 years old and had a tumor the size of a large
watermelon on his right leg. When he first got sick,
the doctors wanted to send him to the Philippines for
treatment. But his cancer was so aggressive, that
before they finished getting the paperwork ready for
him to travel, SST was dying.

As soon as I walked into the children's ward that
morning, the nurses asked me to visit SST and pray
with him. They knew he did not have much time left
and were worried about him. I went into SST's
hospital room and sat in the plastic chair beside his
bed. He had the sweetest smile and thickest black
hair I had ever seen. SST listened closely as I told
him how he could invite Jesus to come into his heart,
and be in heaven with Jesus forever. I held SST's

hand as we prayed together. His mother prayed along with us, and was very thankful that we had come to visit her little boy.

Matthew and I took a small radio, a Gospel of John, and some toy cars up to SST's room the next day on our way back home from church. SST's parents and older sisters were all in the room with him, and we prayed together. A few weeks went by and SST got worse. He was in so much pain and the tumor kept growing. Whenever I would visit him, I would run my fingers through his hair and pray for him, wishing that there was something we could do to help him.

As soon as the doctors felt SST was strong enough to survive surgery, they took him to the operating room and amputated his leg. For the first time in weeks SST slept peacefully. He stayed in the hospital a little while longer, then he got to go home to Wichap. We all hoped that the cancer would not come back, and that SST would keep getting better.

Several of the boys at Kinisou Baptist in Wichap were friends with SST in school and knew where his family lived. Nanas, the young owner of our guide-dog Osenimu, told me that he went to visit SST at his house after he came home from the hospital. SST showed him the Bible and radio that I had given him, and said that as soon as he got better he wanted to come to Sunday School with all his friends. I asked Nanas to take a message to SST's mama that Matthew and I would like to come by and visit them after church the next Wednesday afternoon.

We finished church early that day so we would still have plenty of daylight left for our special visit. Several of the boys wanted to go with us, and Nanas took his position as our visit coordinator and SST's best friend very seriously. Nanas and his dog, Osenimu, led the way as we walked single file down the narrow path through overgrown grass, past several tin shacks and around the corner to the small house where SST's family lived. When Matthew and I finally stepped inside the front door, there was SST sitting on a little bed in the corner of the room. He had been looking forward to our visit for days. I sat beside him and put my arm around his thin shoulders while we all talked together. SST's mother told him to show us the scar where the doctors had amputated his leg below his hip-bone. We talked about church and Sunday School, and SST's eyes lit up to think that one day soon he might be strong enough to come with us.

We brought SST a bucket of cookies and some juice boxes, and his mother gave us each a coconut. Before we said goodbye, Matthew prayed and thanked the Lord for bringing us together again. Later that week, I bought SST a dry erase board with colored markers so he could have something to do during the day. Christmas was just a week away, and we made plans to stop by SST's house on Christmas Day and take him his presents.

The next Saturday when we were visiting at the hospital, I had just finished leading a family to the Lord in the children's ward when Alisha came to get me. SST was back in the hospital, struggling to breathe. The doctors said that the cancer was back, but this time it was in his lungs. There was nothing they could do for him except keep him on oxygen and try to make him as comfortable as possible.

My heart fell when I heard the news. I went down

the hall to SST's room. He was doubled-over in the bed, breathing through an oxygen tube in his nose. His uncle had just finished setting up a small electric fan, trying to give SST as much air as possible. My dad walked with me into the room, and began to pray. While he was praying, I reached over and ran my fingers through SST's hair like I did before when I would visit him in the hospital. Immediately, SST looked up at me and reached out his hand for me to hold. He saw Matthew standing in the doorway and smiled. I held SST's hand in mine and prayed for him, that the Lord would help him to have peace and not be in pain. Finally, I gave his hand one more squeeze and turned to go. His mama, Isinta, was standing behind me. She looked so sad, all I could do was give her a hug and promise that we would be praying.

The next day, Sunday morning around five o'clock, SST went to heaven. Just before he died, SST prayed to Jesus and asked that if it was true that he was Jesus' boy and belonged to Him, then please let him be in peace. After church, Matthew and I went by the hospital to see his parents who were waiting in the small house outside the morgue. Isinta told me that all SST ever talked about when they were at home was getting better so he could come to my Sunday School class. She was so thankful when I gave her copies of the pictures we had taken at their house the week before, and said SST's funeral would be two days later, on Christmas Eve.

I had ordered blue and red straw cowboy hats for my kids' Christmas presents, and on Christmas Eve I took one of the red-trimmed hats with me. A few of the ladies from church rode with Matthew and me in the truck, and we joined the long procession of cars that followed the ambulance all the way from the hospital to Wichap. SST's coffin was a small plywood box covered in light purple material. His mama had dressed him in his best church clothes, and all his brothers and sisters wore matching light purple dresses and shirts. I ran my fingers through his hair and said goodbye to SST one last time, and put his little straw cowboy hat inside the coffin.

****

The next day we drove back out to Wichap for our Christmas Day service at Kinisou Baptist. In Chuuk, Christmas is considered a time to go to church all day rather than a time to be at home with your family. Our kids had a Christmas pageant and quoted verses they had worked hard to memorize, and we sang several Christmas carols. They all looked so cute dressed up as different animals, shepherds, angels, wisemen, and of course Mary and Joseph. The little girl who played Mary held the baby doll very carefully, and rarely took her eyes off him. After the program, Bertina was thrilled when I told her that she could keep the baby doll for her very own. She told her friends, "I just knew that Andrea would give him to me!"

After the service, Matthew and I passed out presents and candy to everybody. The kids loved their cowboy hats and toys, and the adults were excited to get different treats and groceries that I had wrapped in Christmas paper. The most prized gift was a huge pack of toilet paper; everybody could tell what it was just by the shape of the package. We had

23

a big church dinner with tasty local food like barbequed reef fish and pounded breadfruit, with enough food left over for everybody to take some home.

I saved out a basketful of Christmas presents for SST's family, and when Matthew and I finally left the church, we stopped by their house to see if they were home. I looked over at SST's grave, and there were his mama and daddy. Everyone else in their family had gone to church, but they stayed home to be by their little boy. They had been crying, but were so thankful to see Matthew and me coming to visit. They told us their plans to build a little shelter out of wood and tin over SST's grave, and we prayed together that the Lord would come back soon. Our own version of *A Christmas Carol* turned out much differently from what we had thought. Instead of being with us in Wichap for Christmas that year, our "Tiny Tim" got to spend Christmas in heaven with Jesus.

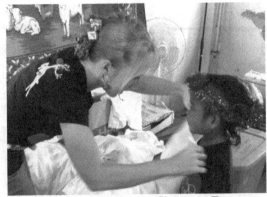

Passing out clothes on Christmas Day

Christmas Program

Christmas cowboy hats and toys for everyone

25

4 UP THE MOUNTAIN AND THROUGH THE WOODS

Many of the moms and dads started coming to church after watching their children come so faithfully. Sometimes we go with our kids to visit their families and pass out tracts. I am always amazed to see what a long trek our boys and girls make each time they come to church. We could never have church after dark; on the way home somebody would be sure to fall off the mountain or get lost in the jungle!

One Wednesday afternoon, Tela came up to tell me that her daddy was home, if we would like to visit him that day. She and her twin sister, Tina, are sweet girls and come to church faithfully. We decided to go as soon as church was over. Since the summer days are longer, we would have plenty of daylight left before the sun set around six o'clock.

I always thought that Tina and Tela lived in one of

the houses down the road from the church, but we got to that point and Tela said, "We live up this way. Follow me!" She was so excited that Matthew and I were coming to her house. We turned off the dirt road and started hiking up the mountainside, following a well-worn path that led through overgrown grass and weeds at an unbelievable slant. At one point we came to a river, and walked across several strategically-placed rocks to the other side where we continued climbing on up the side of the mountain. Thankfully, there was always a breadfruit tree or palm tree nearby to hold on to in case I started to lose my balance!

We heard a loud, familiar pounding sound echoing down the mountain, and I asked Tela if her brothers were making *kon* (pounded breadfruit). The girls told me that their family works together every day to make enough *kon* for their mama to sell in town. What an enormous job!

Finally we reached a high point where we could look down the mountainside into a grassy ravine. Tela said, "That's our house!" Suddenly, she was no longer in front of me, but had managed to climb down a ninety degree drop and stood smiling up at me, waiting for me to follow. I had to laugh and wondered how in the world I would do this in my narrow jean skirt. Somehow I managed to sit down on the top ledge, then stretched out one foot to step onto the first rock below. I slowly eased my way down to the bottom of the cliff, hopped over the last few stepping stones and arrived at Tela and Tina's house.

Their house was a one-room plywood shack with a tin roof. A big pile of rocks were heaped together outside the door in place of a front doorstep. Tela patted one of the boulders in the yard and told me to sit down and rest. All natural lawn furniture! Behind the house was a palm leaf lean-to, where two guys sat pounding breadfruit on a wooden slab. Their job was to pound the boiled breadfruit until it turned into a huge mashy mess, namely *kon*. Then Tina and Tela's older sisters would shape the *kon* into lumps the size of small shoeboxes and wrap them in leaves. Breadfruit that is prepared this way can last for several days. If it happens to sour, some people seem to enjoy it even more.

Tela and Tina's daddy came outside to talk with Matthew, and Matthew gave him a Gospel of John and invited him to church. The girls and I sat together and enjoyed the view of the ocean from that high up. When it was time for us to head back down the mountain, the girls' father told them to take us down via the mango tree. Instead of going back the way we came, we walked down another muddy trail that led away from their house, past a rushing river and over more slippery stepping stones, until we came to a huge fallen mango tree. Tela scrambled up onto one of the branches and stood on the tree trunk, patiently waiting for me to climb up after her. We held our hands out to each side to keep our balance like tightrope walkers, walked down the length of the tree trunk, hopped onto one of the lower branches, and carefully made our way down to the ground. From there it was just a short walk to the bottom of the hill and we were back on the main road that leads back to the church. Another exciting missionary adventure accomplished.

Tela and Tina on their 12th birthday

Best friends

5 LITTLE GRAVES

Probably the saddest sight to see is the grave of a little child. Thank the Lord for the hope we have in Jesus, that all children go to heaven when they die. Some of the Chuukese church leaders began teaching their people that babies who die will go to hell if their parents are not faithful church members. Immediately after hearing this, we wrote a tract called "All Babies Go to Heaven" and started passing it out on visitation. I also translated Dr. J. Vernon McGee's book, "Death of a Little Child," that he wrote after his own daughter died, so we could give it to parents who lose a child. At the end of the book is a simple Gospel message and the sinner's prayer to receive Jesus, so that parents can be saved and know for sure they will see their children again in heaven.

One day, I noticed that BR had not been in church or Sunday School, which was very unusual because he always came and never missed a service. I found out that his family had gone to live in another village closer to town for a while, and I hoped we would get to see them again. A few weeks went by, then we heard the sad news that BR's little brother OJ had become very sick and died suddenly. The family brought OJ back to Wichap to be buried. That Wednesday after church, Matthew and I walked up the mountain with BR to visit OJ's small grave. BR and his little cousins gathered around and Matthew said a prayer; then we took a picture together beside the grave. I have never seen so many sad faces.

We gave copies of Dr. McGee's book about the death of a little child to OJ's parents and grandparents. They were all very thankful, and read and cried through their books many times.

****

One Saturday morning when we walked into the children's ward at the hospital, we heard a heart monitor beeping and a little boy trying to breathe and crying for his mama. That was my first time to meet 6 year old Wilipo and his mother, Mano. Wilipo had been born with heart trouble, and he was about as sick as a little boy could be. I waited outside the room until he calmed down a bit, then I went in to pray for him.

Over the next few days, I kept going back to the hospital to check on Wilipo and see if he was better. One afternoon, I was able to witness to his mother and she prayed with me to receive Christ. I took Mano and Wilipo a portable radio, and from then on whenever I visited them, Wilipo was lying quietly on the bed listening to the radio. Mano told me that every Saturday night after listening to Dr. McGee's sermon that I interpret in Chuukese, Wilipo wanted her to turn up the radio loud so he could pray during the invitation. His second favorite program was Alisha's daily morning exercise. Wilipo would lie on his hospital bed and try to lift his legs and raise his arms like Alisha was telling him to do on the radio.

Wilipo seemed to be getting better, and the doctors took him off the heart monitor. But, they knew it was just a matter of time before he would have a relapse. The people in charge of referring patients started getting the paperwork ready to send Wilipo to the Philippines for treatment. Then one day when I went to visit him, his room at the Chuuk Hospital was empty. The doctors had sent Wilipo home until he was cleared to travel on the plane.

Mano and her husband had eleven children, and little Wilipo was number ten. I knew everybody must have been glad to have their mama and brother back home from the hospital after so many weeks! Their family lives way up on top of the mountain in Epinup, the village next to Wichap. Casey, one of the teenage girls who comes to church, is related to Wilipo's family. I asked her to take a message for me to Mano that Matthew and I would like to come by for a visit one afternoon. Casey came back with Mano's reply that Wilipo was still too weak to leave home and come to church, but they would love to see us again.

We made plans to visit Wilipo the next Wednesday, but on Sunday I heard the worst news: Wilipo died unexpectedly on Thursday, and his family had buried him on Saturday. Of course I wanted to drop everything immediately and go up on the mountain to visit Mano, but that Sunday it was pouring rain and I knew we would not be able to make the climb. Instead, I handwrote a letter to Mano and gave it to Casey to deliver for me. I told Mano how sorry I was to hear about Wilipo, and if the weather cleared up, Matthew and I wanted to come visit his grave that Wednesday. In Chuuk, visiting a person's grave is considered even more important than being with them when they are on their deathbed. I hated that I missed seeing Wilipo one more time, but at least we could see where he was buried and say goodbye.

Casey told me that ever since the funeral, Mano just sat by Wilipo's grave and cried. When Casey gave her my letter, Mano cried even more and said she would be waiting for us to come. Thankfully Wednesday afternoon was bright and sunny. When Matthew and I got to church, the kids were already there waiting for us, as usual. We left everybody playing volleyball and coloring with several mothers in charge, and Matthew and I went with Casey to visit Mano.

We drove down the dirt road that leads through Wichap and into the next village, Epinup. We went up one steep hill and down another, around several twists and turns, until Casey finally said that was as far as we could go in the truck. Matthew pulled off to one side of the path, and we climbed out of the truck and began hiking up the mountainside. Casey was obviously a pro at mountain climbing! She buzzed up the muddy trail in her flip-flops without missing a step. I walked behind her and Matthew brought up the rear. A few times he had to give me a push if I started to lose my balance. At one point, we looked to the right and saw a huge swamp in the valley below, full of deep, murky water and overgrown trees. Another time, the hill was almost at a ninety-degree angle, and we had to get a foothold and pull ourselves up to the next rocky ledge with our hands.

Finally, after what seemed like hours but was actually about twenty minutes, we reached the very top of the mountain. Casey pointed to Mano's house just ahead of us. Mano and several of her daughters were sitting together in a little shack outside their house where they cooked rice and other food over a wood fire. Right outside this cook house was a tiny grave. Someone had spread an empty rice sack like a blanket over the muddy mound of dirt, and lined the grave all around with stones.

Mano was so happy to see me. She showed me the pocket radio that I had given her and Wilipo in the hospital, and told me again how much Wilipo had loved listening to the radio. I asked her about when he died, and she said that the Wednesday before, she asked Wilipo if he would like to go to children's church with Andrea. But he was not feeling very good, and asked his mama if they could go on Sunday instead. The next day, he got so sick that his family carried him down the mountain and took him to the hospital. He died that evening.

Before he died, Wilipo asked his mama to pray for him. Mano told him, "You know how to pray; why don't you pray first, and then I'll pray?" So Wilipo bowed his head and closed his eyes, and prayed to Jesus like he had learned from listening to the radio. Mano prayed after him, and then Wilipo told her, "Mama, I'm going to sleep now, and if I don't wake up, don't worry. I'll be alright." He went to sleep within minutes, and never woke up.

I told Mano, "Isn't that amazing? The last face Wilipo saw on earth was Mama, and the first face he saw when he woke up was Jesus."

Passing out Gospel tracts and toys to the little patients

Sharing the Gospel with a new mother

What a great group of people on hospital visitation

Each week we pass out around 500 tracts

Alisha in the children's ward

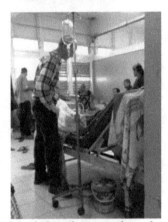

My dad in the surgical ward

Matthew witnessing at the hospital

ANDREA COLSON

6 A LASTING IMPRESSION

A grandmother in our church told us that when she was a little girl, Baptist missionaries came to Wichap for the first time. She grew up learning about Jesus and the Bible, and prayed to receive Christ when she was a young girl. She is thankful that now the children in Wichap have the same opportunity, and looks forward to the day when these boys and girls are grown and our church is full of men and women who grew up loving Jesus and learning the Bible.

One day, a few weeks before Christmas, a kind American man in his sixties drove into our yard. He looked so much like my grandpa, who had passed away a few years before, that at first it was hard for any of us to think rationally and welcome our unexpected guest. The man's name was Ron Allen, from South Carolina. Back in the seventies, Ron and his family had lived in Wichap as missionaries and helped start Kinisou Baptist Church. After being away from Chuuk for over thirty years, Ron's dream to come back and check on the ministry in Chuuk had finally come true.

I honestly cannot say who was happier to meet the other, our family or Ron Allen! What a privilege to meet one of the first missionaries to Wichap. For Ron Allen's part, he told us that for all the years since he left Chuuk, he had been convinced in his heart that he was a failure as a missionary. Now, to come back and see for himself that the ministry in Wichap had continued on was almost overwhelming.

During the week, Matthew took Ron Allen around to meet the folks who knew him and his family years ago. Several of the municipal policemen remembered Ron Allen and his sons. They proudly said that when they were little boys, they went to Sunday School with Missionary Ron Allen and his family and learned about Jesus for the first time.

On Sunday morning, Ron Allen preached at Kinisou Baptist Church and Matthew interpreted. After the service, everybody filed by to shake Ron's hand and give him a flower lei. What a special day! I remember thinking at the time, "Lord, thank You that Kinisou Baptist was still alive and well when Ron Allen came back!" The Lord truly does all things well.

****

One of the most amazing ministries the Lord has made possible for us here in Chuuk is our radio ministry. There is no better way to reach families in their own homes day after day, across the many different islands both inside and outside the Chuuk

Lagoon. From six o'clock in the morning until ten o'clock at night, people can tune in to our FM station and hear different programs, Bible lessons, sermons and songs. We record all the music and programs ourselves, and everything we play on the radio is in Chuukese. Alisha plays the keyboard for the folks at Bible Baptist Church in Nantaku, and they take turns singing solos and group songs. At Kinisou Baptist Church in Wichap, we set my handheld digital recorder on the pulpit and record families singing specials with guitars and ukuleles. Everyone looks forward to Sunday evening when each new song recorded that week is introduced live and plays on our radio station for the first time.

All Chuukese people can pick up a ukulele or guitar and play a song. Bisina, the older lady from Epinup who brings all her grandchildren with her to church, asked if I might possibly be able to help her get a ukulele. She said, "I know many songs, and if I had a ukulele I could sing them on the radio!" I bought Bisina a ukulele from Amazon.com, and after a few weeks it came in the mail. She was absolutely delighted, and she kept her promise. The next Sunday she and her family got up and sang a special with their new ukulele, and that night it played on the radio for everyone to hear.

One of the men in Wichap likes to write songs using the words from our tracts, or from a sermon he listened to on the radio. He plays his ukulele and sings about Jesus being the only way to heaven, and that we cannot receive eternal life by being good. When Matthew preached about what Baptists believe, he wrote a song using the acrostic for "Paptist" in Chuukese. It was a hit!

Minoru is another grandfather from Bible Baptist Church in Nantaku where my dad is the pastor. He got saved after listening to the radio, and started bringing his family to church. For years Minoru had lived a wild life, but after he received Christ, the Lord changed his life and he became a completely different person. He comes faithfully to church and hospital visitation, and has led many people to the Lord. All week long Minoru practices a song to sing on the radio that week, and he comes to church early on Wednesday afternoon so he can record his song while his grandkids play on the playground. At first, none of Minoru's relatives and friends from his home island believed that Minoru had become a Christian and sang on the radio. Several times a week Minoru would call and ask us to play one of his songs; he had a friend with him who needed to be convinced that the stories were true. Minoru really was different and actually did sing on the Baptist radio station.

Once when Minoru was invited to speak during a meeting with his extended family, he stood up in front of the room full of men and held up his Bible. He said, "You all are my friends and brothers, who have known me since I was a boy. You know that in the past, I would have stood here with a beer can in my hand or an empty liquor bottle. But today you see me holding God's Word instead. Jesus has changed my life, and I am not the same man anymore." Minoru preached the Gospel to the men at that meeting and passed out the tracts he had taken with him.

Minoru and his wife, Tomiko, have gone with Matthew and me on all our mission trips to the outer islands. When we were on Pollap, Matthew saw

Minoru writing in a notebook at the end of the day. He discovered that Minoru had been faithfully keeping a diary during each mission trip we went on together. He liked to write down the day's routine and how the church meetings went, how many people he was able to lead to the Lord that day, and what kind of local food he ate.

When Matthew and the men worked together to change the roof on our church building in Wichap, Minoru and Tomiko asked if they could go along and be the cooks. They were so excited to take a field trip and have a part in that big project. One afternoon Minoru looked down the hill and saw a friend of his from years ago walking along the road. He called Miwa's name and told him that he should be coming to the Baptist church on Sundays. Miwa started coming to church, and one Sunday afternoon he prayed with Matthew and invited Jesus into his heart. He was baptized a few weeks later, and now he too is singing on the radio and bringing his grandchildren with him to church, just like his friend Minoru. What a difference Jesus has made in these men's lives!

****

Much of our time every day is spent working on our different radio programs. Our station is on the air every day from 6am to 10pm. We have an 85ft tower outside our house that is connected to our Elenos transmitter, which broadcasts what is playing on our radio station's desktop computer.

My sister, Alisha, translates stories and novels into Chuukese, and types them up so she can print them in book form. For our radio listeners, Alisha reads from a book that she has written and adds background music and sound effects. Her daily story time is more of a production than a program, and people listening to Alisha's stories on the radio say they feel like they are watching a movie. Everybody gets very caught up in the lives of the people in Alisha's different stories and hates to finally hear the last episode. But the next day she will start reading from another book, so soon our listeners are just as involved in the new story and its characters.

Alisha has a daily exercise program that plays each weekday morning at seven o'clock. Many of the ladies especially enjoy exercising with Alisha on the radio every day. One time a friend told me that every morning, her grandmother turns up her radio so loud that it echoes through their house. When Alisha says, "Now, everybody, lift your hands up high above your head," her grandmother makes a face, raises her arms and moans, "Oh, oh, oh!" Then when Alisha tells everyone to stretch out one leg, she follows obediently and groans her way through the rest of the exercise program. Her grandchildren asked her why she keeps on exercising since it hurts so much, and she told them emphatically, "Because it feels good when I'm done! You should try it sometime, then you would be strong like me!"

Another fan-favorite radio program by Alisha is the daily cooking show. She tries to keep her recipes and instructions simple, since most of our listeners do not have an oven, but cook outside over open fires. One man proudly told us that he and his wife have prepared every single recipe they have heard on the radio. Another man calls us on the phone every time we play Alisha's recipe for "No-Bake Cocoa

Mounds," a cookie you can make in a pot on the stove (or campfire). He always wants to make sure he has the ingredients and instructions just right so that when he goes home from work he can explain to his wife how to make him those Baptist cookies!

Of course, Alisha's most important translation project has been translating the New Testament into Chuukese. Missionaries and their Chuukese helpers have attempted to translate the Bible in the past, but there has never been an accurate translation of the New Testament until now. With each book in the New Testament, Alisha also translates Dr. J. Vernon McGee's study outline and introduction for that book. Several folks in church help with proof-reading, and everyone is amazed at how clear and perfect Alisha's Chuukese translation of the Bible is. What a blessing to finally have the exact Word of God in this obscure island language for people to read and study!

****

Alisha translates the Bible, and Matthew records himself reading two Bible chapters at a time to play on the radio. Every few months he will have read through the entire New Testament for all our radio listeners. Matthew also teaches a daily Bible study program using Dr. McGee's Thru the Bible commentaries. It is great to know that Dr. McGee's Bible program that is broadcast around the world in many different countries and languages, is also being broadcast in Chuukese.

Matthew and a few of the men from church record a talk show during the week and have a round-table discussion about different questions or topics from the Bible, such as "What does it mean to be born again?" This more casual style of radio program has caught the attention of many new listeners, and now everyone is curious to hear which question will be answered or discussed this week. We also record my dad's and Matthew's Sunday sermons in church to play on the radio the next week.

My dad, Jody, teaches a daily Bible program. He addresses many problems common in Chuuk, such as drinking, living together without actually being married, and giving your children away. When he taught verse by verse through the minor prophets, people kept commenting how relevant the lessons were for life in Chuuk. One man said that every evening when he gets home from work, he and his wife go into their room and shut the door and listen to Missionary Jody's lesson for the day. His only wish was that he could write faster and take better notes, because he likes to share what he learns from the Bible with his family and friends.

My mom, Terry, has a devotional program that plays each day. She also manages the daily radio schedule, and makes sure the programs play at the correct times. In addition, she schedules all of the music, which includes exchanging older recordings for more recently recorded songs. Of all the jobs involved in running a radio station, I think being in charge of the program schedule is the hardest!

Matthew, Alisha and I record headline news stories from around the world every day, and Alisha tells the daily weather and tides report. Everyone likes to hear what is going on in the rest of the world. I think knowing the world news makes people in Chuuk feel less isolated and more connected to the outside world.

I have several different programs that play every day. Unlike Alisha, who takes the time to type out her programs so she can print them in books, I just open a book written in English, turn on my microphone, and record in Chuukese what I am simultaneously translating in my head as I read.

Our first story time of the day is "Nurse Cherry Ames," which plays each weekday morning at six thirty. Every day, I read for a few minutes from one of Helen Wells books about Cherry Ames, a young nurse who has exciting adventures and cleverly solves mysteries. In her book *Cherry Ames, Chief Nurse*, Cherry is an army nurse stationed on a small island in the Pacific. How funny to think it might have been an island near Chuuk!

My next program plays around lunchtime. This is usually a story with a religious theme, such as the *At Home in Mitford* stories by Jan Karon; or, a missionary story, like Darlene Diebler Rose's *Evidence Not Seen*. My personal favorite is John G. Paton's *Thirty Years Among the Cannibals*. John Paton was one of the first Christian missionaries to bring the Gospel to the South Pacific, and he would travel between the different islands by ship, just like we do now.

Another story I did for the radio was the memoirs of Henry Obookiah, the first person from Hawaii to receive Christ. Henry was born in the late 1700s and heard about Jesus when he went to America as a teenager. He planned to return to Hawaii and take the Gospel to his people, but he became sick and died suddenly. His American friends published a book about Henry's testimony and included many letters that he had written. The first missionaries to go to Hawaii were young Christian college students who read Henry Obookiah's book and went to Hawaii in his place.

One of the letters Henry wrote was to a young friend from Hawaii. Henry explained the Gospel to him in such a way that any islander could easily relate and understand, and he asked his friend to give his heart to Jesus before it was too late. His letter was so persuasive and clear that I translated it into Chuukese and made a tract for us to pass out. I love to think how even from heaven, Henry is still helping to reach the island people he cared about so much.

Probably my most popular radio program, besides the sermons I translate by Dr. J. Vernon McGee and others, is Nancy Drew. When I was a little girl in Hawaii, I read every Nancy Drew book available at the Wahiawa library. Many times I would finish a book in one day, they were so exciting! How fun to get to enjoy Nancy's adventures all over again by sharing her stories with my Chuukese audience.

Another fan-favorite, especially among the kids, are the stories from Uncle Remus about "Brother Dog" and his animal friends. Originally these stories are about Brer Fox and Brer Rabbit, but since most folks in Chuuk have never seen a fox or a rabbit I had to adapt to our situation.

Running a radio station and recording all the music and programs definitely takes time and hard work. But the end result makes it all worthwhile! I cannot count the times we have heard about someone who prayed to receive Jesus after listening to our station. Many times at the hospital, Alisha or I will go up to a family and start to talk, only to have them recognize our voices immediately. "You're the one who talks on the radio!" Our Chuukese radio fans do not know about asking for an autograph, but they do want to shake hands and say thank you, and tell us how much they enjoy listening to our station. Even the folks in our church have become radio stars! One elderly man in the men's ward asked if we could please tell Minoru to come and sing him a song. He loved listening to Minoru's songs on the radio and knew he would feel better if Minoru would sing to him in person.

Of course, with so many songs and programs playing through the air around them, everybody wants a radio! In Wichap, I told the kids that if they would read the Gospel of Mark, I would give them a radio of their own. Alisha had recently finished translating Mark at that time, and had printed it by itself in a booklet. I soon had quite a list of boys and girls who had read the Gospel of Mark. Some of them read Mark's Gospel as a family. KJ, our young TB patient, told me that each night his whole family gathered together in their house to listen to his mama read Mark by candlelight. I am not sure how many candles it took, but a few nights later, they had finished reading the book of Mark and were ready to get their family radio. KJ's little brother KM was so proud the day he finally finished reading Mark and got his prize! Every Sunday he brings his radio with him to church, carefully wrapped in a hand towel, so Matthew can put new batteries in it for him.

****

Radio ministry is a wonderful way to leave a lasting impression in many lives. Taking trips to the different islands in Chuuk is wonderful, but at the most, you can only be there with the people for a few days or a week. But when you give someone a radio, they can listen to Christian music and Gospel preaching day after day. And radio waves travel so far! People who live on islands up to 160 miles away from the Chuuk Lagoon, where our radio tower is located, tell us that they can tune in to our station on their home island. If you would like to get involved in our radio ministry, I explain in the last chapter of my book how you can make a donation for us to buy radios. A Christian company makes portable radios that are perfect for Chuuk: they are solar powered and come pre-tuned to our station. These radios cost $10, a small price to pay for an investment that will last forever if a listener prays to be saved.

Ron Allen and Matthew visit the Mayor and municipal police

Recording a new radio program in my office

Learning a new song during Sunday School

How exciting to get your very own radio

Recording a song together

Sunday morning choir at Bible Baptist Church

My dad, Jody, preaching at Bible Baptist Church

Matthew preaching at Kinisou Baptist Church

Little radio stars

Alisha plays the keyboard while the children sing

My mom, Terry, records and edits dozens of songs each week

Tomiko and Minoru singing a duet

7 GOD ANSWERS PRAYER

Chuuk is actually made up of many tiny islands scattered over hundreds of miles of water. The islands inside the Chuuk Lagoon where we live are mountainous, but the islands outside the reef are coral atolls just a few feet above sea level. Some of the outer islands are less than a mile long and barely half a mile wide, but with a population of several hundred people.

My first experience on the open sea was when Matthew and I went to Satowan for a friend's funeral. Satowan is in the Lower Mortlock region, about 180 miles away from the Chuuk Lagoon. That first trip opened up a whole new ministry for us, and since then Matthew and I have taken many trips to Chuuk's outer islands. Thanks to friends and supporters who give generously to our mission trip fund, we can charter a small local ship and travel across the ocean to remote islands and share the Gospel. Our mission team is made up of Chuukese adults from our two

Baptist churches on Weno. Each one has been saved and baptized, and is actively involved in soul-winning visitation each week. Each time we get back from a trip to the outer islands, everybody is ready to pack up and go again! Many of our folks are from the lagoon islands, and never dreamed they would one day be able to travel outside the reef and help take the Gospel to other Chuukese people who have not yet heard.

Our first few mission trips were to different islands in the Upper and Lower Mortlock regions, south of the Chuuk Lagoon. In my heart, I hoped that one day the Lord would open the door for us to go west to the Western Caroline islands, where the people are even more isolated and cut off from outsiders.

Several years after we started our radio station, a woman and her daughter from the western island of Pollap came to Weno to stay with relatives. The woman's name was Piriki, and her daughter was Anechen. Piriki's nephew had come to our island to go to school, and one afternoon when he was walking home, a group of guys from an island in the lagoon attacked and killed him. Nothing was ever done because this is Chuuk, and murderers often go unpunished. Piriki was afraid for her own son, who was also in Weno to go to school, so she and Anechan came to stay with him. Someone living in their relatives' house had a radio and was playing our station. On Saturday night, Anechan and her mom heard the sermon that I interpreted for Dr. J. Vernon McGee on the Parable of the Sower. During the invitation at the end, they both prayed to receive Christ. The next morning, they walked to our church in Nantaku so they could meet our family in person, and tell us how they had been saved the night before while listening to the radio.

Anechan and I soon became good friends, and she would tell me stories about her home island, Pollap. The men (and many of the women) still tie pieces of material around their waist in the traditional loincloth fashion. They speak Chuukese with such a strong accent, that it is almost like another dialect. Like the other western islands, Pollap is considered closed to outsiders. The chief and the mayor are in charge of the entire island, and if they do not personally invite a person or group to come to Pollap, then those people are not welcome. One afternoon, I asked Anechan how we could possibly take a mission trip to her island. She replied that the mayor would have to invite us to come. The people would follow his lead, and we would be accepted and welcomed.

Months passed, and Anechan left Chuuk to go live with her relatives in Guam. We met other people from Pollap at the hospital on Saturday morning visitation, and they were always very kind and open to the Gospel. Alisha gave some ladies from Pollap several of the books that she has written in Chuukese, and they were thrilled.

The ladies all knew Anechan's family, and told us how the folks on Pollap had been listening to the CDs of radio programs, songs and sermons that we had given Piriki, Anechan's mom. Later, Piriki sent us a letter with a friend who was traveling to our island by ship. In her letter, Pikiri said that every Sunday she gathered her family and friends together in her house so they could listen to a sermon by Dr. McGee on CD. Alisha got more CDs ready, and we sent them to Piriki by a returning ship, along with batteries for her CD player.

One day I received a Facebook message from Jill, a Christian lady in Texas. She shared that her husband, Lanny, had visited Pollap a few years earlier to try out his ham radio equipment from that remote spot. Jill wrote:

> *"In the year 2004, my husband Lanny traveled to the island of Pollap accompanied by the Deputy Chief of Mission at the FSM Embassy in Washington, D.C. His reason for going there was to set up a temporary Ham Radio station...*
>
> *"While he was there he asked the Deacon on the island if there was anything he could do for him and he said send me Bibles in the Chuukese language. We have tried several different avenues to try to find Bibles in the language to get to the Deacon but to no avail.*
>
> *"As I was praying this morning, I felt that I should search the internet for missionaries to Micronesia and that is when I found you..."*

Jill and Lanny asked if I knew of any Bibles available in the Chuukese language that they could purchase to send to the Deacon on Pollap. I replied that my sister Alisha was currently working on translating the New Testament, and had already finished several of the Gospels. At that time, we had John, I John, II John and III John available together in one book, with the Gospel of Matthew in a separate book. Our new friends from Texas quickly went to Amazon.com and ordered several dozen copies of each Gospel, plus a few of the Christian novels Alisha has written in Chuukese. They sent the boxes of Bibles and books to our address in Chuuk.

When the books came in the mail, I packed them all in a big waterproof plastic tub, and added Gospel tracts, candy for the children, and yarn for the ladies. (Chuukese women like to use colorful yarn to decorate handicrafts they make from woven palm fronds, like fans and sleeping mats.) Our ship captain friend, who had taken us on all our mission trips, was getting ready to leave for the Western Caroline islands and would be passing by Pollap, so Matthew asked him to deliver our box for us. We addressed the container to the mayor of Pollap, and included a letter explaining who had sent this gift to his people.

A week or two went by, and our captain friend came back to Weno. He had not gone as far as Pollap after all, but when he reached the nearest island, Tamatam, he radioed to the people there to send a boat out to the ship. He needed them to deliver a box to Pollap from the Baptist church on Weno.

Several weeks passed with no word. One morning, I was praying in my room and asked the Lord to please make a way for us to take a mission trip to Pollap. I prayed that if it was God's will for us to go, he would send the mayor and the island leaders to invite us to come to their island. This would be a clear sign from the Lord that He wanted us to go. I was still praying, when I heard someone calling me to come. Apparently, we visitors! Several men from an outer island, dressed in their best Sunday clothes, had come to visit the Baptists. You probably know without my saying, but the men who came to visit us that day were the mayor of Pollap, the island chief, and my friend Anechan's uncle. These men had just arrived on the ship, and wanted to thank us in person for the box of Bibles we had sent. They said that when the box first reached their island, the Catholic priest and the mayor opened it and looked to see what was inside. The priest saw the Bibles and the tracts and told everyone that God's Word had come to their island at last. He and the mayor went all over the island passing out Gospels of Matthew and John, the tracts, and the other gifts that we had sent. Everyone was so happy! They just had one request. Could we please come visit their island and preach the Gospel to the people on Pollap? We would be welcome any time, whenever the Lord made it possible for us to come. The island would be waiting for us.

Mayor Edward from Pollap comes to invite us to his island

Visiting our friends Lanny and Jill in Dallas, Texas

8 ROUGH TIMES

Before being invited to go to Pollap, we had been planning a trip to an island in the Mortlocks that we had not yet visited. A few days before we were supposed to leave, the ship broke down and all trips were canceled until a mechanic from Japan could come and fix the engine. A month or so went by, and finally the ship was running again. We got ready a second time, and radioed to the island to let the people know that we were on our way.

Then the day before we were scheduled to leave on our mission trip, the weather was terrible and there was news of a tropical storm headed our way. The wind howled and rain poured down almost nonstop, and the waves were ten feet and higher. The weather station on Guam issued a high surf advisory for Chuuk, and said that any travel across the ocean or even between the islands in the lagoon could be dangerous. We all prayed that if it was the Lord's

ANDREA COLSON

will for us to go on our mission trip as planned, He
would calm the storm. I specifically asked Him to
please remove the red warning sign on the weather
report if we were supposed to go. The next morning
when we got up and checked the new report, there
were TWO red warnings at the top of the page
absolutely advising against any ocean travel due to
strong winds and high surf. We took that as our clear
answer from the Lord to postpone our trip a second
time.

Soon after, the men from Pollap came to visit us,
and we found out what the Lord had in mind all
along. They indicated the best time for us to come to
Pollap would be during the summer. Surely, we could
manage to visit the Mortlock island we had been
trying to get to for so long, and then plan our trip to
Pollap when we got back.

The week before we were scheduled to leave for
the Mortlocks, two ladies from the education office
came up to the house to ask us to postpone our trip
so that they could use the ship instead. They had to
send teachers to all the schools on the outer islands to
test the eighth grade students who were graduating,
otherwise none of them would be able to register for
high school. Of course there was no way we would
could say no to their request. The Education
Department promised to allow our mission team to
travel with the teachers, since they would be visiting
the same island that we wanted to go to in the
Mortlocks. But a few days later they changed their
plans and said that if we went with them, they would
leave us behind on the island to wait for another ship.
We would have to wait a month or longer to return
home!

Obviously it was not working out for us to go south, so I asked the ship's owners if we could instead use the ship to go to Pollap as soon as the teachers got back to Weno. At first they wanted to charge over one thousand more dollars, but thankfully they agreed not to charge us any more money if we planned to be gone only five days instead of an entire week.

Back when we were first planning to leave on the ship, Matthew and I went shopping and bought the food we would need on our trip. When our mission trip kept getting cancelled or postponed, I put the food in boxes, covered the boxes with a blanket and left them in a neat pile in the corner of my bedroom near the foot of my bed. My thoughts were that whenever we ended up going on our trip, at least we had our food and were ready to leave. Surely everything would keep until we finally went on our next mission trip. After all, it was mostly cans of stew, ramen noodles and Snickers candy bars.

One evening I made sandwiches for supper, and remembered a can of Pringles potato chips that was in our box of trip food. I went to my room to get it, and made a horrifying discovery: termites had somehow found the boxes of food in my room, and had eaten their way through it all. But they were still not content, because they had continued eating their way underneath my bed through all my shoes and sandals that I had carefully put away until my next visit to America. I no longer owned a single pair of dress sandals! Even the clothes I had stored in plastic bags had been ruined by termites.

Thankfully, my dad and Matthew were able to come to the rescue. The termites had not gotten into my wooden bed frame, thank the Lord, but everything else was history. I still do not understand how I managed not to hear those greedy bugs chewing and chomping their way through whatever they pleased, right underneath my nose!

****

Our trip to Pollap was finally right around the corner. Since the summer months are usually very calm, I hoped that July would be a beautiful time to travel across the ocean. This would be our first time to go to the Western Caroline islands, and I had heard stories about how much rougher the waves were on that side. I got more and more nervous the closer the time came for us to go. To get ready to leave on the ship again and again, only to find out that we were not going after all, had been more stressful than I realized. We all hoped and prayed that this time, nothing would keep us back, and we would be able to go to Pollap as planned.

Finally the week came. We were scheduled to leave for Pollap on Sunday afternoon. That Saturday morning, the lady from the ship office called to say that the teachers from the education office had taken longer than they originally thought to test the students, so the ship would probably not return to Weno until Monday or Tuesday. Her suggestion was that we cancel our trip and try again later. At first, no one at the ship office would radio the ship's captain to ask that he return immediately. But they finally contacted him, and he agreed to return to Weno by Sunday. That meant that the soonest we could leave for Pollap would be Monday afternoon. Once again, a delay that could not be helped.

ANDREA COLSON

9 ON OUR WAY AT LAST

On Monday morning Matthew started taking our supplies down to the ship. There were ten people on our mission team, which included Matthew and me, and eight Chuukese men and women from our church, who were saved and baptized and joined us on visitation each week. Ten people from Pollap were also traveling with us to their home island. Including the captain and crew, there would be about twenty-six people on board the ship. We had told the mayor and other island leaders that we could bring supplies and food for their people. Flatbed trucks pulled up to the dock with bags of rice and flour. Containers of gasoline were lined up side by side around the edge of the lower deck. On the upper deck, all of our blue five gallon jugs of drinking water were tied to the side rail. Soon the ship was full, and it was time for us to get onboard and head out to sea. Matthew and I had already said goodbye to Alisha and my mom at the house. My dad was waiting with us at the dock, and he led us all in prayer. I walked across the plank and climbed up to the top of the ship towards the back and sat on the plastic chair that I brought with me. All my church friends seemed to have stayed below towards the front, and the strangers traveling with us came up to where I was sitting and made themselves comfortable. I had passed around the seasick pills about thirty minutes earlier. Since I had not eaten much that morning because I was nervous, I took my medicine on an empty stomach. That is never a good idea, ever.

As I was sitting there in my plastic chair, trying to keep out of the way of all the ladies and girls from Pollap crowding in around me, I could feel the panic start to rise in my throat. Right then my cell phone rang. Alisha and my mom were calling to see how I was doing. All I could think to say was that I wished I was anywhere in the world but on this boat! Immediately, my mom knew that something must be wrong, and asked me about the medicine I had taken. I went down to where our cooler of food was and got myself a Snickers candy bar and a bottle of water. Surely that would make everything better!

By this time the sailors had untied the ropes from the dock and the ship started slowly on its way, gently rocking back and forth. With the recent engine trouble, the captain decided to only go about six knots, which is even slower in real life than it sounds on paper. I stood by the guard rail at the back of the ship and watched my dad and everyone on the dock start to disappear from sight. I realized that there was no going back. Ready or not, we were on our way to Pollap, and I was going to be stuck on this tossing and turning boat for at least the next 24 hours. I know it was the medicine making me have such a panic attack, but I cannot possibly explain the sinking feeling I had all through me as home got farther and farther away. There is no experience quite like losing sight of land and home as you head out to the open sea. You are on your way to visit a primitive outer island you have never been to before, knowing that you are responsible to share the Gospel with the people who live there, because you are the one God has chosen to go.

Thankfully, I was not by myself at all! Matthew was right there, and he could tell I needed to get a grip. He ran back and forth from the upper to the lower deck, getting out the camp stove to heat up some water and make me a cup of ramen noodles. He made sure I had all the flavored water and oranges I could handle, and even let me borrow his sunglasses that were a different tint than my own and easier to wear on the water.

My cell phone had a signal all the way to the reef and about thirty minutes beyond, out on the open sea. Alisha checked the internet for what to do in case of seasickness or a feeling of panic on board a ship. My mom tried to redirect my thoughts by talking about my next trip to the U.S. and everything I planned to do and see there. Thank the Lord, by the time we lost the signal, the medicine had begun to wear off, and I was feeling much better. Matthew and I moved our plastic chairs to the lower deck and sat near our church friends. I tried to stay awake as long as I possibly could, but like it always does, there came the time when at last I had to gather my courage and stretch out on the deck and try to get some sleep. I always hate that initial part of actually lying down, in case the sudden change in position might make me get seasick. But thankfully, I was able to survive the long night without having *that* complication and did eventually fall asleep. The Lord really does know your limits, exactly how much you can handle at one time.

The night finally ended, and the next day around lunchtime we could see Pollap in the distance. What a relief to know we were almost there! And to think that at least the next time we got on this ship, it would be to head back home. I prayed in my heart that the people on Pollap would open their hearts and listen to the Gospel, and that we would be able to lead many of them to the Lord. Then all these rough times would be worth it, no matter how difficult.

Our home island Weno disappears in the distance

Land ho! After 24 hours at sea

Pollap Island

10 POLLAP

As usual, the ship anchored out away from the island, and young men came out in boats to help us get to shore. I knew for certain that we were at the right place, because all the men and boys were wearing pieces of material wrapped around their waist instead of pants or shorts. They were very kind and helpful, making sure the ladies were able to climb over the side of the ship and down the ladder into the motor boat waiting below. The sailors opened up the hold, and one of them jumped down inside among all the boxes and bags of rice. He asked me to point out what needed to be brought to shore first, so that we could go ahead and have our first children's meeting. I knelt at the edge of the hold and hung my head over the side, trying to identify which plastic tub had the candy and tracts and which black plastic bag held my felt board.

The waves were choppy and the sky was overcast

as we rode to shore in the motor boat, but I could feel my excitement begin to rise. When we got closer to the island, I saw kids running from all directions to stand along the beach among the palm trees, jumping up and down and waving to us. What a beautiful welcoming committee!

The water was too shallow for the boat to go all the way up to the sand, so I carried my flip-flops with one hand, slung my purse over my shoulder, and stepped down into the warm, crystal-clear knee-deep ocean water. Waiting on the beach to greet us with a big smile and a strong handshake was Mayor Edward, wearing nothing but a bright red loincloth. My friend Anechan's aunt was with him, and gave me one of the biggest hugs ever. She had heard about me for so long, that the moment we met in person there was an instant connection between us. We felt like we had known each other for years.

Our friends from church who had gone in the first boat were sitting on the grass drinking coconuts outside a big cement house built right beside the ocean. Apparently during the school year this was the head start (Kindergarten) building. The ladies had cleaned it up and brought in mats and pillows so our mission team could stay there together. You can imagine how relieved I was when I found out our house actually had an indoor bathroom with a roof, a door that latched, and a toilet bowl! The one drawback was a plastic United bag nailed up over the screen window instead of a curtain. But the plastic bag was opaque enough, so no one standing outside could actually see in.

In one corner of the bathroom was a deep well that had no cover or lid. When I cautiously looked over the edge of the well, the hole seemed deep enough to reach the ocean floor underneath the island! The water level was low, probably thirty feet or more from the top of the well. Instead of a bucket at the end of a rope, someone had taken a ship's buoy like a round plastic ball, and cut out a triangle section on one side so the buoy could be used to scoop up water. The ladies all seemed to know exactly how to toss this buoy into the well at just the right angle so that it immediately filled with water. Then they would pull the long rope back up, hand over hand, and pour the water into the wash basin that sat in the middle of the floor. The small bucket beside the wash basin was used to dip water to flush the toilet or take an island-style shower, pouring bucketfuls of cold water over yourself.

Thankfully, my friends always made sure the washbasin had plenty of water whenever it was my turn in the bathroom. The few times I tried to get water out of the well myself, the buoy seemed to revert to its original purpose and would just float on top of the water.

After everyone in our team had a chance to take a shower and get something to eat, we went over to the big open-air gym just a short walk away from the house where we were staying. America had built this gym and a dispensary on Pollap many years ago, and the gym was big enough for everyone on the island to come and sit inside. We decided to have all our meetings and activities right there in that perfect spot.

The young boys from Pollap were always ready to help carry our things, and one of them rang the bell so all the children on the island would hear and come to our Bible story time. I started by playing my ukulele and leading the kids who were there sitting on the floor in front of me to sing one of Chuuk's most popular songs, "Kot A Nenetiw" (based on John 3:16). I knew the sound of kids' singing would go even farther than the bell, and everyone would be curious to come see what the Baptists were all about.

We kept singing and soon the gym was filled with men, women, boys and girls. I taught everybody a new song that I had written, the Christian-Chuukese version of "Pearly Shells" that our kids back on Weno loved. The Pollap boys and girls picked it up in no time, and later before we left the island, they asked me to write down the words so that they would be sure to always remember and never forget it.

Then I told a Bible story about Jesus from the New Testament. I explained the Gospel; how we can have eternal life in heaven if we believe in Jesus and ask Him to come into our hearts and forgive our sins. After the lesson we all bowed our heads and closed our eyes, and many of the children and adults prayed to receive Jesus as their Savior.

Then the ladies helped pass out coloring pages and crayons, and everybody got to color to their hearts' content. We passed out bright colored cross necklaces that I had ordered on Amazon, and the men and women tried on reading glasses to see which number was the best fit for their eyes. After the kids finished coloring, the ladies helped them line up and we passed out clothes, flip-flops and toy cars. The older teenagers and adults got the extra mission team shirts that I had brought along as gifts, and they were just as excited as the kids!

By this time it was late in the afternoon, so we all went back to the house where we were staying to take a short break before the evening. We were planning to show the "Jesus" film, translated into Chuukese, on a big screen. The people of Pollap would be able to watch this movie for the first time.

Evening came, and while Matthew set up the screen and the projector, I brought out my digital recorder. I asked the teenagers and kids who had come early to let me record them singing a few songs for our radio station. They were thrilled, and one young man volunteered to play my ukulele and lead them. Our radio listeners back in the Chuuk Lagoon would be so excited to hear these songs recorded on Pollap!

The gym was soon packed with men, women and children who came from all over the island to see the movie about Jesus. Some of the young people stood around the outside and watched, because there was no floor space left inside the building. It was too dark to see the looks on their faces, but I could tell from hearing their reactions just how much they were enjoying this big-screen movie that was actually in Chuukese! During the invitation I could hear people praying to receive Jesus, and before everyone went home, the men on our mission team made sure that each person who came got a Gospel tract.

The next morning, Matthew and Aurelio took the antenna and portable radio down to the beach. They were attempting to get our radio signal from 160 miles away. It was low tide, so they were able to walk out on the sand. Sure enough, our radio station came in loud and clear! The song playing at the time happened to be one by Mayleen, Aurelio's wife. Mayleen had stayed behind on this trip because she was expecting a baby. Aurelio admitted hearing

Mayleen's voice made him homesick. How exciting to know that even from this far away, with a good antenna and radio, the people on Pollap would be able to tune in to the Baptist station and hear all the music and programs that play every day.

Later that morning, the mayor and his friends led us from house to house, making sure no home was left out. We passed out tracts, the Gospel of John, and the sports bracelets we brought that had "I ♥ Jesus" printed on one side, and "I ♥ Baptist Radio" on the other.

In addition to having our mission team make contact with each family on the island, Matthew made plans that day to meet with the island police and young men. He had brought Taekwondo uniforms for those interested in a session in self-defense. The few men who did not receive a uniform were just as content to kick, block and punch in their loincloths. How funny to see those with a uniform stuff the brightly colored material wrapped around their waist into the waistband of their new white pants. They could not wait to learn!

Matthew trained them in the basic moves, then showed them what to do if an attacker came after them with a machete or a baseball bat. He gave everyone a turn to kick the target or take the bat away when he swung at them, and each time the men would clap for each other and laugh and tell their friend, "Good job!"

The only one disappointed that day was the mayor. By the time he and Roy and Minoru got back from their last visit, Matthew had already started training the men and all the uniforms were taken. He must have had his heart set on getting one of those white jackets and matching pair of pants.

After the self-defense class the ladies and I taught the children and passed out the rest of the candy and clothes that we brought with us. We all agreed that if we ever came back to Pollap, instead of bringing clothes we should just bring bolts of material for new loincloths! For the handicraft time, the kids got to decorate paper sacks with glue and glitter and make puppets. That was their first glue-and-glitter experience and they loved it!

That evening everyone came early to the gym, and after we sang several songs together, Matthew preached the Gospel. It was very quiet, and everyone listened closely. He explained that we can have eternal life by putting our trust in Jesus. Many people were saved that night.

We ended our time with a big screen showing of scenes from the TV miniseries, "The Bible." Everyone especially enjoyed the opening that depicted the Creation.

So far I had not had a chance to go swimming in the beautiful ocean water, but that night when we got back to the house, Matthew and I got our towels and went outside to the beach. I may have been breaking an island superstition by going swimming at night, but I did not care! I climbed over the rocks in my dress and sat down in the waist deep water right there by the shoreline. What a wonderful way to relax and unwind after a long, hot, busy day.

Welcoming smiles

Teaching the children on Pollap a Bible story

Minoru shows the boys how to use glue and glitter

Hut-to-hut visitation

The mayor led us around the island

Matthew training the police

This sweet lady prayed with me to receive Jesus

Catching our radio signal from 160 miles away!

11 GOOD-BYE FOR NOW

The next morning, it was time to get back on the ship and head home. Thank the Lord, we had been able to do everything we came to do on Pollap; our candy and tracts were gone, we had visited in each home, preached the Gospel and showed the Jesus film. Matthew decided to leave the radio and antenna set-up with one of the senior police officers. He and his family lived in a big local-style hut complete with a sand floor and a roof made out of palm leaves. His little girls were playing in their family's dug-out canoe with one of the dolls I had given them. Matthew showed Dominic how to use the radio, and he called for one of his sons to bring him a chair. He planned to sit out there on the beach and listen to the radio station the rest of the day. When Matthew first tuned it in and caught our signal, we could hear Alisha's voice as she gave the daily weather report back home on Weno. I admit, I got a sinking feeling in my stomach when I heard her voice saying, "Today, the wind will be strong, about 20 mph, and we should expect rain. The waves will reach eight to ten feet." Uh-oh! And we were about to be out there in the middle of those waves!

An elderly lady lived in a small tin shack just a few steps from the house where we had stayed. Every time I would walk by, she would stop me and say hello. That last morning when she saw me, she called me over to say good-bye and gave me a big palm-leaf fan. I sat beside her and shared how she could pray and invite Jesus to come into her heart. She listened seriously and when I asked, she said she would very much like to pray and receive Jesus. We prayed together and shook hands one last time. Later that morning while I was sitting and talking with my new friends, a boy came up and said his grandmother had sent him over to give me this present. I opened up the plastic bag and found a beautiful piece of woven material that the people on Pollap used to make in the olden days on looms that sailors brought them. This piece of material was meant to be worn rather like a wrap-around skirt, the more traditional way of wearing a loincloth. It was bright yellow with blue and red stripes, such a special gift to remind me of my time on Pollap and all that God had done to bring us there and safely back home again.

All the little kids were so sad to see us go, and asked when we were going to come visit them again. Looking at their faces I thought about my Sunday School boys and girls back home in Wichap. I wished that one day these sweet boys and girls would all be able to listen to the radio station and learn about Jesus every day. The radio is such a wonderful way to reach people right where they are, at home in their grass hut or tin shack, on an island that is not on most maps and certainly not on any globes!

The boys helped carry our bags out to the motor boat that would carry them to the ship. The sailors were loading up and getting ready to pull up the anchor. Matthew and I had come to the island in the last boat, and we left the island in the last boat. I shook hands and patted little shoulders and waded out to the boat.

The waves were steadily getting higher, and as we headed out to the ship I saw an amazing sight. An old-fashioned sailing canoe had left Tamatam, the island just a few miles away, and was coming to Pollap. The mayor who was with us in the boat said they must be coming to see what the Baptists brought! The only thing modern about the sailing canoe was that the sail was made from a navy blue tarpaulin instead of woven coconut fibers. I managed to take a few pictures whenever the waves would lift up our motor boat so that I could catch a glimpse of the canoe and the men sailing it.

We reached the ship at last and climbed up the ladder to get on board. Matthew and I decided to start out at the front of the ship on the lower deck this time, rather than in the back. I passed around the seasick medicine to the ones who wanted it (except for me! I had learned my lesson last time and decided not to take any). Two boats from Pollap circled the ship a few times to see us off, then headed for home.

The sky overhead was iron-gray and covered with clouds. It started to rain, a steady drizzle and first and then a huge downpour. We seemed to be traveling in the middle of a thick fog and could only see a few feet past the side of the ship. Alisha's report was correct, the waves were definitely eight to ten feet high. The ship was not as heavy because we had left all the bags of rice and flour on Pollap. Each time a really big wave came at us, the front of the ship went up off the water and slammed back down again. It felt like any minute the ship might literally break in two.

The sailors keep a canvas tarpaulin stretched across the front deck, but the rain and waves were splashing in on all sides and we were all getting soaked in spite of the tarp over our heads. I sat with my knees huddled to my chest and tried to hold my pink flower umbrella over my head to keep off some of the driving rain, but the wind was so strong my umbrella kept turning inside out. My sweet friend, Elimy, must have noticed my teeth chattering. She opened up her plastic container with everything she might need during her trip, and handed Matthew and me a humongous comforter bedspread. Who knows where she had come up with that! We gratefully put Elimy's blanket over our heads, and for a while, it helped protect us from the wind, but soon it was sopping wet and incredibly heavy. The old saying is right: there is absolutely nothing fun about a wet blanket.

The rain kept coming down in torrents, the waves continued to crash and pound, and we still could not see very far beyond the edge of the ship. I finally took two Tylenol and two Benadryl and crawled in between the other ladies who were trying, like I was, to not roll over the side of the ship when it would sway first to one side and then the other.

It is unbelievably cold out on the ocean in the

middle of a thunderstorm. Matthew was freezing in his wet jeans and jacket and got out our sleeping bags. Being the good brother that he is, he unzipped my bag and covered me up with it like a blanket. Thankfully I had found a place to lie down underneath the middle of the tarpaulin and out of the pouring rain. Matthew decided to use his own sleeping bag the right way, but the minute he got inside and zipped it up, the ship pitched to one side and he went rolling with it. The polyester material of the sleeping bag against the fiberglass deck was like waxed paper on a playground slide. Thankfully, Matthew was able to grab hold of something and stop his fall, or we most likely would have had a man overboard!

At first, no one seemed seasick. But suddenly, Firstleen, who I thought was asleep, sat up. She had such a shocked look on her face that I asked if she was okay. She told me that she felt dizzy, so I felt around for my purse and got her some medicine. Thankfully her dizzy spell passed, and she never actually got seasick. But, during the night, I could hear the folks from Pollap who were traveling with us start getting sick. There are few sounds as bad as hearing someone throw up into a bucket, again and again and again.

The night seemed like it would never end. But eventually morning came, as it always does. When the sun was up, we could see the outline of the mountain islands in the lagoon way off in the distance. Thankfully, the waves had calmed down by then, and everybody began to wake up and move around and get excited about reaching the pass in the reef and, finally, our island.

God had taken us safely to Pollap and back home again. I could hardly wait to take a hot shower and then send out an email with pictures from our trip, letting all our friends who had been praying for us know what had happened and how the Lord had answered all our prayers in so many ways.

Loading our supplies

Such cute, capable helpers

Pulling up to the dock on Weno

ANDREA COLSON

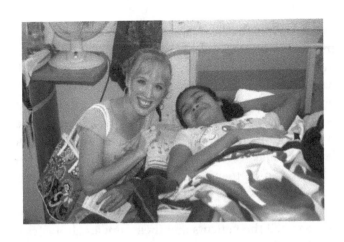

12 ANESLY

Probably the one nice thing about visiting at the Chuuk State Hospital each week is that you get to meet people from many different islands and villages. I say "one" nice thing, because the hospital is definitely not a place you can enjoy visiting. It is very dirty and run down, with betel juice stains in every corner where people chewing the nasty concoction spit without thinking. The bathrooms are a horror, and usually the halls are flooded with water and lined with garbage that has been piled up for days. Once I walked past the nurses' station just in time to see an enormous rat's tail disappear around the door, and roaches are a common sight.

The doctors and nurses do their best to take care of their many patients, in spite of such terrible surroundings. The young men in Chuuk get drunk and shoot each other with homemade arrows, made out of nails or filed-down pieces of rebar and other metal. One of the Filipino surgeons has removed thousands of these arrows and saved countless lives in the time he has been in Chuuk. Many of the adults have diabetes, so if they get a cut on their foot or hand, it can quickly become infected and never heal, which means that often the doctors have to amputate. A large number of children and young teenagers have heart trouble. Entire families contract diseases like TB or even leprosy. With so many people sick and hurt and in pain, a trip to Chuuk Hospital could be very discouraging if it were not for the fact that we go there to tell the patients and their families about Jesus and how they can go to heaven.

One Saturday I visited a family from the outer island of Mokur. This was one of the first times I had met people from that island, and could tell that they must have recently arrived on the ship. Some of the girls still seemed a little seasick and wet with ocean water, like they had only just then come to shore. I shared the Gospel with them and they all prayed with me to received Christ, even the girl who was sick and lying on her side in the hospital bed. Her name was Anesly, and she had such a bright happy smile on her face. I promised to come back later and bring her a radio so she could listen to the music and programs.

When I visited Anesly and her mother again, I found out why Anesly was in the hospital. About two weeks earlier, a typhoon had passed by Chuuk on its way west toward the Philippines. When the storm reached Mokur, the small tin and plywood house where Anesly was hiding with her family collapsed on top of them. Everyone made it out unhurt except for Anesly and her sister. Anesly's sister was cut up rather badly but was okay. But poor Anesly's back was broken, and she was paralyzed from her waist down. Anesly's dad and brothers dug the two girls out from underneath the pile of debris that had been their house. When the ship came by their island a few days later, Anesly's family carried her onboard and brought her across the ocean to the Chuuk Hospital here on our island in the lagoon.

There was nothing that could be done for Anesly at the Chuuk Hospital, and one of the local doctors recommended her family take her back home to their island. But the Filipino doctor wanted to send Anesly to the Philippines where the surgeons could at least set her backbone that had been broken in two, and make it possible for her to sit upright. Until now she was only able to lie on her back or her side.

Weeks went by, and it seemed like Anesly's name would never get put on the list of uninsured patients to be sent to the Philippines. I even tried to talk to the US Embassy and see if anything could be done to get Anesly out of Chuuk, but the answer was no. The assistant director of the hospital is a member of our church, and I talked to him about Anesly's situation. He immediately started looking into what could be done, and one afternoon came by the house to show me a paper. On it was the names of all the people being sent to a hospital in Manila for treatment. Anesly's name was right there in the middle of the list!

One family member was allowed to travel with Anesly and stay with her at the hospital in the Philippines. Her parents decided that it would be best for her dad, Akilino, to go. Anesly and her family were so happy and thankful to God for taking such good care of them, especially now that they had received Jesus as their Savior and were trusting in Him. I put some of my shirts and a few other things in a backpack and took it to Anesly for her trip. This was going to be quite an experience for Anesly and Akilino; neither of them had ever been on an airplane before or seen any part of the world outside of Chuuk.

The Filipino doctor at the Chuuk Hospital made Anesly practice sitting up in bed every day, so she could sit upright in an airplane seat long enough to reach Guam, and then Manila. An ambulance would be waiting there to take her and her dad to Medical City. The afternoon they were supposed to leave, I went down to the airport to say goodbye. Anesly arrived at the airport in an ambulance. She was wearing one of the new shirts I had given her. Her dad carried her backpack along with his own. Whatever they had in those two small bags was all they were taking with them on this long trip. Anesly and I prayed together one last time, and the airport worker opened the gate in the chain link fence so the ambulance could drive out to the waiting airplane. Anesly's mother had been able to hold back tears as she said goodbye. But she sobbed into a t-shirt as we stood together, watching Anesly being helped into a special wheelchair, then carried up the steps into the plane. She was sure that this was probably the last time she would see her husband and daughter alive.

I had the name of the hospital in Manila and finally managed to get through on Skype. The switchboard operator transferred me to Anesly's room, and Akilino answered the phone. He was so happy to hear a voice from home! I asked how they were doing, and if he had been able to buy something to eat with the money I gave him before they left. Akilino said, "Someone tried to show me how to use the thing they call an 'eleva-tor', but I don't think I can do that on my own." He was sleeping on the floor underneath Anesly's bed and sharing some food from her hospital tray. I tried to get him to ask the nurse to show him once again how to get downstairs to the cafeteria. Akilino just laughed and said that was okay, he would be fine. He was embarrassed to ask for help, especially when it was almost impossible to communicate anyway because he only understood a few English words.

Anesly wanted to talk, and her dad handed her the phone. She tried not to cry when I asked her if she was homesick, and I told her not to worry. I would find some Baptist friends to come visit her and her dad and make sure they had everything they needed.

My first attempt to contact some missionaries I knew of from my parents' mission board did not work out, since they were leaving for America the next day. I wrote my own mission office in Houston to ask if they could please put me in contact with any CMC missionaries near Manila. Then, while I waited to hear back, I did a Google search and discovered the Facebook page of a Filipino pastor of a large and very active Baptist church right there in Manila. I wrote Pastor Abante a message over Facebook and explained the situation. Within minutes I heard back from him, such a kind message promising to send two of his staff members to the hospital right away to check on Anesly and Akilino. He said he would keep in touch and let me know how my friends were doing, and make sure that they were being taken care of.

A few hours later I got another message from

Pastor Abante, this time with a picture of Anesly lying in her hospital bed (still wearing the same shirt she had on when she left Chuuk), and a very pretty Filipina lady standing beside her. A couple from Lighthouse Baptist Church had gone to visit Anesly and her dad, brought them food and took Akilino to exchange money and buy food at one of the many places available on the ground floor of the hospital. Before they left they made sure Akilino would be able to get around on his own, even in the infamous elevator, and prayed for Anesly. When I talked to Akilino on Skype that night, he told me how the Baptists had come to visit and about all that they had done for him and his daughter.

Anesly's sister had a cell phone, and she and her mother were staying with relatives in a village on the other end of our island. Using some MacGyver-like skills thanks to my family, we were able to call and get Anesly's mother on the phone. Then I held the phone up to the microphone that was plugged into my laptop for Skype calls, and Akilino and Anesly were able to talk to their family back home in Chuuk. When he was talking to his wife, Akilino went into "CB radio" and kept repeating the same phrase over and over again: "This is Anesly, Anesly, Anesly. We are alive, alive, alive!"

The Lord had still other Christians in the Philippines lined up to take care of our Chuukese friends. A Filipino Facebook friend responded to my message saying that his brother was a nurse in the same hospital where Anesly was. That night when the brother's shift ended, he went up to visit Anesly and her dad and sent a picture to show us that they were doing okay. He must have taken them food because there was a big take-out bag from KFC on the bedside table.

My friends at CMC contacted their missionaries in the area, and I heard from Dan Tessin, a missionary in a town several hours from Manila. He was very kind and ready to help in any way possible. Dan's sister-in-law, Rosemarie, and her husband, Joy, who was a Baptist pastor, lived right around the corner from the hospital. Over the next few weeks that Anesly was in the hospital, right up until the day she and her dad left to come back home to Chuuk, Pastor Joy and Rosemarie would visit them almost daily. They would take homemade food and even ice cream, share the Bible and pray and show the love of Jesus to their new island friends. When Rosemarie found out that Akilino had been washing his and Anesly's clothes in the bathroom sink, she and the ladies in her church gathered together some clothes for them both. Every time I would call on Skype, Akilino would tell me all that Pastor Joy and his family were doing and how very thankful he was for them. He had heard that Baptists really love Jesus, and now he knew it to be a fact! Anesly became instant friends with Pastor Joy and Rosemarie's little daughter, who was heartbroken to find out that Anesly was not going to be in the Philippines forever!

Before Anesly and Akilino left the Philippines, Missionary Dan Tessin and his daughter, Jennifer, flew to Manila and went to visit them in the hospital. By then Anesly had been moved to a room on an even higher floor, and Akilino said just looking out the window made him dizzy! What a blessing to hear about Dan and Jennifer's visit and see the pictures they sent. The Lord had done amazing things during those weeks and answered many prayers.

When the plane came to Chuuk bringing Anesly and her dad, I went down to the airport to meet them. There was Anesly's mother leaning on the same chain link fence, but this time she could not have been more happy and excited! We took a picture together outside the airport with Anesly, who was now able to sit up in a wheel chair thanks to her surgery and physical therapy, and a special back brace from the Filipino doctors. She and her dad were full of stories about their new friends and how the Lord had taken such care of them while they were away. Above all, they were thankful to be home again at last, safe and sound and on their way back to familiar third-world island life.

Chuuk Hospital ambulance drives out on the runway so Anesly can be carried onboard the plane

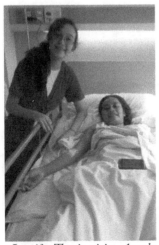

Jennifer Tessin visits Anesly in Manila hospital

Welcome home!

ANDREA COLSON

13 TYPHOON MAYSAK

The last Saturday in March 2015, we got the news from the Guam weather station that a typhoon was heading to Chuuk and would most likely hit our islands the next day, on Palm Sunday. We immediately began announcing about the typhoon on our radio station so people would know what was coming and be prepared for what might be ahead.

We did not turn off our radio transmitter that night as usual. Instead we stayed on the air, giving live updates as new reports were released from Guam or the typhoon watch center in Hawaii. My mom chose a special lineup of songs, and introduced each one with a Bible verse and encouraging words about how God was able to take care of us even through such a huge storm. My dad and Matthew took turns praying on air, and when the wind was howling loudly and the rain was pouring down Matthew read Psalm 91 from the Chuukese Old Testament.

All night long the storm kept coming closer and

closer to our islands, but instead of hitting us during the night it slowed down between Pohnpei and Chuuk, getting even bigger and stronger before continuing on toward us. Of course we had already cancelled Sunday services in both our churches, and told everyone to make sure they stayed in a safe place and did not go outside. The storm was on its way.

By this time the island power had gone off, and we were using our little gas generator with extension cords stretched across the backyard from the generator to the house. One extension cord went to the radio transmitter room, and the others went inside to our computers, a light or two and the refrigerator.

On Palm Sunday morning when the typhoon was still a few miles outside our lagoon, I remember being so nervous that I went into our dark kitchen and started pulling out the ingredients to make cake donuts. The birthday cakes I had made the day before were stacked neatly on the shelf in their bakery boxes, just in case a miracle happened and I managed to make it out to Wichap that day after all.

Our biggest concern, besides hoping no one got hurt, was for our radio tower. It was supposed to be able to withstand winds up to 70 mph, and Typhoon Maysak had already reached sustained winds of 95 mph and greater. Around nine o'clock that Sunday morning, the first part of the storm hit our islands in the Chuuk Lagoon. My family and I all sat around the living room, collectively holding our breath each time we heard the tower outside creak and pop as the wind and 160 mph gusts slammed against it. Our tin roof sounded like it was flapping up and down over our heads, ready to tear off the nails and go flying through the air any minute. What a shock to see the mango tree in our front yard topple over and fall directly in front of our house. The wind had pulled that enormous tree up by its roots, and thankfully the Lord kept it from landing on our house.

I remembered too late that my bedroom window was facing the direction of the wind and rain, and ran back to see what damage had been done. Months before I had taken down the glass panel windows that had been in my room, and now all I had between me and the outdoors was security screen, mosquito screen and a curtain. Rain was drenching my room and everything in it, and the floor was completely flooded with water. Thankfully the electricity was off!

I sat on the bed trying to hold my curtain in place at the bottom corners of my window and keep out the driving rain, but it was almost pointless. The curtain kept billowing like a sail and hitting me in the head, and I was soon as wet as everything else in my room. All I could think about was how much this felt like being back on the ship in the ocean in the middle of a storm, trying to keep the rain off with my pink umbrella. My mom and dad came to the rescue with a shower curtain and blanket, and my dad nailed them both up over the inside of my window. Later when the wind calmed down a bit he boarded up my window from the outside.

I could not shake the déjà vu feeling of being on a ship at sea; having my window boarded up with plywood made my room dark and musty-smelling, just like the hold of the ship. That night after the storm was over, my bed and sheets were still wet from the rain that had poured in that morning. I curled up in the middle of the mess and tried to go to sleep. The roar of the generator and the smell of gas fumes definitely added to the overall feeling of being back onboard the ship. I admit my room did seem to be pitching and tossing from side to side for quite a while, but eventually I fell asleep in spite of myself and the all-too-familiar circumstances.

****

The first half of the storm came and went. Immediately the wind and rain stopped and a warm misty fog filled the air and covered our island. That was my first time to actually experience the eye of a typhoon, quite an eerie feeling. People began coming out of their houses, and we could hear the sound of hammers pounding and axes chopping as men tried to nail their tin roofs back on or clear away the branches and trees that had fallen everywhere. No one understood that the storm was not over.

So we went on the air on our radio station and explained to everyone listening in that the storm was not over, and they needed to gather their families and find a safe place to hide until this second part of the typhoon finally passed us by. Thankfully our radio station was still on air, because of the backup generator and transmitter and the fact that our tower was still standing strong.

Around twelve o'clock noon, the wind started to howl like a freight train speeding through the valley beside our house, and rain began coming down in a torrent. This second half of the storm was much fiercer than the first half. Tin was flying and trees were falling all around, but our radio tower survived the storm.

That afternoon around three o'clock, the typhoon had officially passed through Chuuk and was barreling toward Yap, another state in Micronesia. Later we saw pictures from the space station that showed just how huge this typhoon had been, reportedly the strongest storm ever to cross the northwestern Pacific before April.

All phone lines and cell towers were down, but some CB radios were still working. Reports began to come in from different villages and islands, and the news soon spread that five people had been killed during the storm. One of them was a little boy from a village on our island Weno. He and his parents were hurrying to reach their relatives' cement house that was safer than their own home. The little boy got there first and was worried when he realized that his mom and dad had fallen behind. They were an older couple and he was their only child. The little boy ran back outside to call for them to hurry. At that moment a piece of tin flew through the air and killed the boy right in front of his parents.

At his funeral a few days later, one friend comforted the grieving man and his wife by telling them, "Your son loved you and ran back to call you to come quickly. Now he is waiting for you in heaven, calling you both to come quickly and join him in God's house where you will all be safe forever."

ANDREA COLSON

Mango tree fell on our church roof

Alisha and I survey the damage during the eye of the storm

Banana trees down all over the island

14 AFTER THE STORM

After the storm was over, Matthew and my dad drove around to check on as many of our friends from church as they could reach. Everywhere roads were blocked by fallen trees, pieces of tin and other debris. Many of the houses damaged were only plywood shacks to begin with, but during the storm they had the roof torn off or part of the outer wall ripped away, and some houses collapsed completely. Mango trees all over the island had been pulled up by their roots, just like the tree in our yard. Banana trees had fallen over and lay smashed down in muddy heaps. The breadfruit trees that were still standing had lost most of their leaves and branches. All the palm fronds on every coconut tree were permanently bent in the direction of the wind, and some of the coconut trees had been snapped in half like twigs.

For days after the typhoon hit, the sky was full of

bats and birds flying around looking for a home. With so much damage to the trees, the bats especially were now homeless and lost. I never thought I would feel sorry for a bat, but I certainly did then.

Before the storm, our islands in the lagoon looked like lush, green, jungle-covered mountains. After the storm our islands were more like dry, brown desert hills, covered with white sticks that used to be healthy trees before the wind stripped off their branches and leaves. Here and there were dilapidated tin-and-plywood shacks that were people's homes; the greenery on the mountainsides used to keep them hidden from view, but now they were exposed for the world to see.

Thank the Lord, everyone from Bible Baptist Church was alive and well and only a few families had major damage done to their homes during the storm. Early that evening Matthew and I tried to drive out to Wichap to check on our friends from Kinisou Baptist Church, but we had to turn back while we were still several villages away. The road was blocked with too many trees; there was no way we would make it out to Wichap that day. Bad news always travels fast, and so far we had heard no news at all from Wichap or Epinup. We prayed for our friends out there and hoped to hear soon how everyone was doing.

The local power plant workers and their American boss worked almost non-stop trying to restore power where they could. The first priority was to get the deep well that pumped water into the hospital tanks turned back on, because the hospital was out of water. I could hear the American man in charge of the work crew shouting directions to his team in English. Alisha and I took one of the birthday cakes I had baked before the storm down the hill to the work crew. I am not sure if the cake helped or not, but thankfully our power was turned back on after only a few days of being off. The telecom workers put the Baptist radio station at the top of their priority list. They had our internet connection back about the same time as our power. What a miracle! How wonderful to be back online to let our friends in America know what was going on and to ask for prayer.

I have hundreds of Chuukese friends on Facebook who live in Hawaii, Guam and the mainland U.S., and my inbox was flooded with messages from people asking if their families at home in Chuuk were okay. On Sunday night we shared each message on the air. Everyone in Chuuk was thankful to the Baptist station for relaying the messages from their relatives in America, and those far from home were relieved to hear how things were going in Chuuk.

On Tuesday after the typhoon, Matthew was finally able to hike into Wichap and check on our church there. Thankfully the new church roof was only slightly damaged, a small hole in the tin toward the back of the building. Coconut trees and mango trees blocked the road all the way through Wichap and Epinup, and people coming into or out of the villages had to climb over and under countless trees and branches.

On Easter Sunday I put on my tennis shoes, packed my purse with Sunday school flashcard pictures, plastic Easter eggs and candy, and was ready to hike to church with Matthew. By then the work crew had cleared away more trees and broken power lines, and we were able to drive further into the village. The walk was not quite as long as it had been a few days earlier. We carried what we could and walked up the muddy village road to our church building on a hill, and only had to crawl over three or four huge mango trees along the way. In fact, one tree was so big that instead of scaling it like a wall, the kids and I ducked underneath and squeezed through the small space between the tree trunk and the ground.

Before our Sunday school lesson, we filled the plastic Easter eggs with candy and I went outside to hide them for an Easter egg hunt. Our boys and girls had never done anything like that before and were so excited! I told them that when I shouted the all clear, they could run outside and grab the first egg they saw, then come back inside the church and sit down as fast as they could. That way we would have enough eggs for everybody to get one. Of course after the first egg hunt, I ended up collecting all the eggs so I could hide them again and give everyone one last thrill. With breadfruit trees and coconut branches all over the place, there was an unending supply of hiding places!

****

The storm seemed to bring out the worst and the best in people. America sent so much help in money and food, that people were able to get food for free and could use their money for other things, like alcohol. Every time you went anywhere, no matter what time of day, you would eventually lose count of the drunks stumbling down the road.

The work crews trying to clear the roads kept having confrontations with families who wanted the big trees left alone that had fallen on their property. They claimed that a ghost lived in the center of each fallen tree, which meant it was taboo to cut up the tree with chainsaws and move it out of the way. Local witchdoctors were busy going from tree to tree to do chants and prayers and chase the ghosts away.

Thankfully, the people in our churches who had been born again had a much different testimony. When the relief aid workers passed out applications for people to fill out claiming what they had lost during the storm, they talked to one of the ladies from our church. The aid worker in charge of filling out the form asked Elimy questions. Did she have enough food or was she and her family hungry? What trees had they lost? Had their house been destroyed? Elimy answered each question honestly. No, she and her family had plenty to eat. A few trees fell but nothing serious, and they would all grow back eventually. Their house was a little torn up but it was okay. The person asking the questions looked up from the form and asked, "What religion are you? You are the first person I've talked to that has been this truthful!" Elimy answered that she was a Baptist and had been born again, and that Jesus was taking perfect care of her and her family.

Typhoon Maysak was a wake-up call in many ways. It was a reminder to us all how quickly life can change, and how important it is that people turn to the Lord and repent while they still have a chance. The storm helped our family to see once again just how much our friends in Chuuk love us. As soon as the storm ended, people were coming to check on us and see if we were okay. They told my mom how much they enjoyed hearing her calm announcements all through the storm, and how listening to the radio station kept them from being afraid and helped them to trust in the Lord.

Day after day, our friends from church came over to help us clear away the mess we had everywhere from all the fallen trees and branches. In just a short time, the mango tree that had been blocking our entire front yard had been reduced to a neat pile of firewood, with just the tree trunk left for my dad and Matthew to cut up using the chainsaw.

Part of my office roof blew off during the storm and after my dad nailed it back in place I went inside to start cleaning up. I discovered that the ceiling panels had come down, too, and the horrible, huge lizards that usually hide between the tin and the ceiling had crawled inside my office and were running around as they pleased! The boys who had been out in the yard chopping wood heard me scream for help and came running. They got all the lizards out, and Matthew put the paneling back in place with screws. Ten-year-old Envin was brave enough to stand on my desk and poke crumpled sheets of paper in the few holes that were left to make sure no more lizards could get through. My hero!

Many houses were damaged during the storm

Some houses were destroyed completely

Driving through the flooded road to check on friends

*Roy and Salo stayed safe during the storm
and listened to their radio*

Climbing over fallen trees to get to church on Easter Sunday

15 LOVE, ATTENTION, AFFECTION

Like many other places in the world, Chuuk is a hard place for children who want to be good and follow Jesus. Many of the teenage boys and men are alcoholics, and domestic abuse against women and children is a major issue. I look at the boys and girls in my Sunday school class and "kinter" week after week, and I pray that the Lord will protect them and keep them safe and help them to grow up to be all that He wants them to be. Probably the most important life lesson we try to teach the children is: No drugs, No alcohol, No cigarettes. How much better to never get started down that dark road in the first place, than to try to quit or give it up.

One young boy told me how his friends in his village, some even younger than he is, are starting to smoke cigarettes and chew betel nut (a narcotic commonly used in the islands), and some have even started drinking alcohol. Erchen said his friends keep telling him to join them, but he says no and stays away from them. I encouraged him to keep saying no and never ever take a drink or do drugs or smoke. He laughed when I said that maybe one day he would be the only old Chuukese man who lived all his life and never touched any of those things. Erchen is ready to rise to the challenge and live his life for Jesus. The Lord has put so many little Erchen's in my life. Hopefully we will be able to continue helping our boys and girls get started early on the right road.

An older Chuukese friend who grew up in Wichap years ago follows my Facebook page and comments often on the pictures I post. Usually my friend comments in English, but after seeing pictures of the boys and girls with their birthday cakes he wrote in Chuukese: "Imagine how these little children would cry unceasingly if they ever heard that you were going to leave them. I know if I was one of these children and I found out that you were leaving Chuuk, I would cry hot tears forever and never forget you. All I can say is, 'Lord, please keep Andrea in Chuuk forever and ever, Amen.' Only God can truly show you how very thankful Chuuk is for your family."

****

A former Miss World who is also a Christian said that all around the world children are the same. All children long for love, attention, and affection. Her words touched my heart; that has definitely been my experience with the boys and girls in Chuuk, no matter which island or village they are from. What a blessing and a privilege to be able to share the love of Jesus with the children of Chuuk, and hopefully teach them the most important lesson in life: how to receive Jesus as their Savior, and spend their lives loving Him and doing His will.

But that is something that all people in the world need to know, no matter who they are or where they are from. On Facebook I shared the link to a sermon by Dr. Charles Stanley called "The Way to Heaven" that I had translated and posted on YouTube. A friend in Belgium, who follows my missionary posts on Facebook, listened to this message and prayed to receive Jesus as his Savior. What a special blessing from heaven that was to my heart, that a person in Europe would get saved after hearing a message that had been translated into Chuukese for our radio listeners here in the islands. Jesus knows the heart of everyone. He is waiting for men and women, boys and girls, to turn to Him and answer His call and receive His free gift of eternal life in heaven.

My dear friend, thank you for reading my book that tells just a small part of what my life is like as a missionary in Chuuk. If you are wishing for peace and joy and security in your own heart and life, I would like to ask that you turn to Jesus and confirm your belief in Him as your Savior and Lord. He came down to earth and died in your place on the cross, to pay your debt of sin and make it possible for you to spend forever and ever with Him in heaven. He knows everything about you, and He loves you more than you can know or imagine. You can receive Him as your Savior and be born again by praying a simple prayer. This is the prayer you need to pray to Jesus if you want to be clean and forgiven, and know for sure that you will go to heaven.

"Dear Jesus, I know that I am a sinner. But I believe that You died for me on the cross and rose again from the dead after three days. Please come into my heart and forgive all my sins, and give me Your free gift of eternal life in heaven. I want to receive You right now as my Savior and Lord. In Your name, Jesus, I pray, Amen."

Maybe you used to dream about becoming a missionary one day, but for some reason life turned out differently and your dreams and hopes never became a reality. Missionary life is not for everyone; maybe the Lord wants to use you to help another missionary who is already on the field serving Him. You can have a part in the life of each boy and girl here in Chuuk, even if you never come here personally or move here as a missionary. Each person who gives to the Lord's work in Chuuk has a vital part in everything that happens here. If it were not for faithful friends and churches who sponsor our family as missionaries, we could not afford on our own to do the work that God has called us to do.

With so many boys and girls (and birthdays!) I always look forward to boxes of new clothes and toys to give away to the children. Nothing you send will be wasted, it is all put to good use and given away almost as soon as it comes. Boxes of toys, clothes and other goodies can be mailed directly to my address here in Chuuk:

Andrea Colson

P.O. Box 819

Chuuk, FM 96942

If you would like to be a partner in the ministry here in Chuuk, you can sponsor me through my mission board in Houston, Texas. Online gifts can be given over CMC's secure website, and whether you give by check or over the internet, you will receive a tax-deductable receipt and at the same time be laying up treasure in heaven.

Central Missionary Clearinghouse asks that checks be written payable to CMC and sent to the mission address in Houston, Texas. You can include a note with your check designating your gift for Andrea Colson in Chuuk. CMC's address is:

Central Missionary Clearinghouse
P.O. Box 219228
Houston, Texas 77218-9228

To give online, visit CMC's website at **http://cmcmissions.org/donate** and use the Click-and-Give option to donate directly to my account. If you have any questions, CMC's toll-free number is 1-800-CMC-PRAY. CMC also has a special mission-trip fund set up for us, so if you would like to give toward the cost of a mission trip to outer islands like Pollap, just designate your gift "Colson Mission Trip Fund."

Our radio station is available online, and you can listen over the internet to the music and programs that are playing on our station in Chuuk. On your computer, go to our radio station's Facebook page under the name "Bible Baptist Radio Station 88.5 FM." Click on the tab that says "Click Here to Listen" and you will hear what is actually playing live on our station in Chuuk. To listen to our radio station over your phone or mobile device, just download the free app called TuneIn Radio and search for "Bible Baptist Radio Chuuk." What you hear playing over our radio station Facebook page or on your phone with the TuneIn app is exactly what is playing over the air in Chuuk at that same time.

I send out email updates and would love to add you to my mailing list. Just email me at **andreainchuuk@gmail.com**

I have a very active Facebook page and post pictures and updates from Chuuk almost every day. Please follow me on Facebook or add me as a friend, and we can keep in touch. My page is Andrea Colson at **http://www.facebook.com/andreainchuuk**

****

Life is good. I have been able to cross the ocean to visit remote islands and teach the children who live there about Jesus. Every week God blesses me with the chance to see boys and girls come running down the dirt road carrying a backpack with the Bible they earned in Sunday school, excited to come to church again. I have Chuukese friends who are waiting for me in heaven. And who knows? They may just be waiting to see you, too. Thank you for praying and for giving, so that I can be what I am, a missionary to Chuuk, Micronesia.

*Telling boys and girls in America how exciting life is
when you are a missionary*

Easter Sunday in Chuuk

AFTERWORD

I had finished writing my book, and we were working on one last proof-reading before I submitted the final version of *Let Them Come* to the publisher. On Sunday, we planned to have the Lord's supper and a baby dedication for M-Son and Merian's new baby girl. Matthew had a terrible cold, but he took some medicine and we headed out to Wichap with a truck full of birthday cakes, Kool-Aid and bread. Several weeks before, I started taking this favorite Chuukese treat to each church service. Most of our folks walk a long way to come to church, and are hot and hungry by the time they arrive. I love seeing the kids' faces light up when I hand them a cup of cold Kool-Aid and a warm roll.

But when Matthew and I got to church that morning, we heard sad news. M-Son and Merian's other child, their little boy, 2-S, had passed away the day before. 2-S was born with heart problems, and had been sick with TB. He was in the hospital for several weeks, but had come home and seemed to be doing better. 2-S loved coming to kinter and church. His daddy, M-Son, always carried him everywhere and took extra-special care of him.

M-Son was waiting for us when we drove up, and asked if Matthew could come with him and have a funeral service for little 2-S before they buried him outside their house. I wanted to go along, but the church was filled with boys and girls who had come early for Sunday school, so I stayed behind while Matthew went with M-Son. I gave Matthew a blue beanie baby teddy bear for 2-S. The little angel loved stuffed animals, and always smiled brightly whenever I gave him one.

Matthew walked up the mountain to the poor, muddy shack where 2-S's family were all gathered together around a small plywood coffin. When Matthew put the teddy bear on top of the casket, everyone broke down crying. In the distance, they could hear the bell ringing for Sunday school. As they were crying over little 2-S's body, his family said, "Andrea is ringing the bell for Sunday school, but you can't go. You can't get your Bible and your backpack and go to kinter with your friends. Oh, 2-S!"

After several minutes, Matthew read some verses and prayed. M-Son and Merian put the blue teddy bear inside with 2-S before finally closing the coffin lid. Later, before they buried him, his family put the rest of his toys on top of the coffin. Matthew had some bags of cement and sand left over after making the base for our radio tower, and he gave them to M-Son for the grave.

To me, this story is a perfect example of what missionary life is like. I will always remember how it felt when I had to stay behind and not go to the funeral of my little Sunday school boy, 2-S, because I had a church full of other boys and girls waiting for me to be *their* Sunday school teacher.

My book may be finished, but the stories and experiences certainly are not. At least, not until Jesus comes, and we are all together in heaven at last.

2-S and his daddy, M-Son

2-S's grave, with his toys and backpack on top of the casket

ABOUT THE COVER

Merty is a good, sweet girl, and the oldest of ten children. Each week Merty helps get her younger brothers and sisters ready and brings them to Sunday school and church. She sits with them to make sure they are good, and carries them when they are too tired to walk home. Merty loves Jesus and has been saved and baptized. Visit my Facebook page to see more pictures and stories of Merty and many other boys and girls here in Chuuk.

ABOUT THE AUTHOR

When Andrea was a little girl the Lord called her parents, Jody and Terry Colson, to go to Hawaii as missionaries. While in Hawaii, the Colson family met people from Chuuk, Micronesia, and in 1997 the Colsons left Hawaii and moved to Chuuk. Andrea, her sister Alisha, and her brother Matthew are each individually supported missionaries with Central Missionary Clearinghouse, and continue to serve the Lord in Chuuk as a family.

Andrea's first book *Reaching the Uttermost Part* and her next book *Let Them Come* are both for sale on **Amazon.com** in paperback and digital download.

If you have any questions or would like to get in touch, email Andrea at **andreainchuuk@gmail.com**

To sponsor Andrea as a missionary, visit CMC's website at **cmcmissions.org/donate** and use the secure Click-and-Give option to donate to Andrea's account on-line.